THIRD EDITION

TOP NOTCH 1

WORKBOOK

JOAN SASLOW
ALLEN ASCHER

with Barbara R. Denman and Julie C. Rouse

Top Notch: English for Today's World   Level 1, Third Edition
Workbook

Pearson Education, 10 Bank Street, White Plains, NY 10606 USA

Staff credits: The people who made up the *Top Notch* team are Pietro Alongi, Rhea Banker, Peter Benson, Tracey Munz Cataldo, Aerin Csigay, Dave Dickey, Gina DiLillo, Nancy Flaggman, Irene Frankel, Shelley Gazes, Christopher Leonowicz, Julie Molnar, Laurie Neaman, Sherri Pemberton, Pamela Pia, Rebecca Pitke, Jennifer Raspiller, Charlene Straub, Paula Van Ells, and Kenneth Volcjak.

Cover design: Tracey Munz Cataldo
Cover photo: Sprint/Corbis
Text design: Tracey Munz Cataldo
Text composition: TSI Graphics

Photo credits: Original photography by Michal Heron. Page 1 Caro/Alamy; p. 7 Action Plus Sports Images/Alamy; p. 9 Alberto E. Tamargo/Sipa USA/Newscom; p. 11 (left) C. Fletcher/Alamy, (middle left) INTERFOTO/Alamy, (middle right) epa european pressphoto agency b.v./Alamy, (right) Antonia Hille/ Getty Images; p. 16 (left) JupiterImages/Stockbyte/Thinkstock/Getty Images, (middle) Courtesy of Matheus Rocha, (right) WaveBreakMediaMicro/Fotolia; p. 17 John Kershaw/Alamy; p. 21 (left) Deklofenak/Fotolia, (middle) JupiterImages/Stockbyte/Thinkstock/Getty Images, (right) Dean Bertoncelj/Shutterstock; p. 27 olezzo/Fotolia; p. 30 (top) Stephen M. Dowell/MCT/Newscom, (bottom) ZUMA Press, Inc./Alamy; p. 49 Maksym Yemelyanov/Fotolia; p. 50 Mitchell Clinton/Alamy; p. 55 (top) Rido/Fotolia, (bottom) silverphotos/ Fotolia; p. 60 Maurizio Martini/Fotolia; p. 62 Cusp/SuperStock; p. 63 John Warburton-Lee Photography/Alamy; p. 66 ellensmile/Fotolia; p. 69 (1) Alexandra Karamyshev/Fotolia, (2) Natalia Merzlyakova/Fotolia, (3) zhekos/ Fotolia, (4) 33333/Shutterstock, (5) Karkas/Shutterstock; p. 72 (3 left) Silver Burdett Ginn/Pearson, (3 right) vetkit/Fotolia; p. 73 (left) Jelena Ivanovic/Fotolia, (middle) serkucher/Fotolia, (right) Alexandra Karamyshev/ Fotolia; p. 75 (left) dell/Fotolia, (middle left) Hemis/Alamy, (middle right) xy/Fotolia, (right) Anton Maltsev/ Fotolia; p. 78 (3) ryanking999/Fotolia; p. 80 Noam/Fotolia; p. 81 Brocreative/Fotolia; p. 92 John Sun/EyePress EPN/Newscom.

Illustration credits: Steve Attoe: pages 10, 17, 35, 58 (bottom), 76; Kenneth Batelman: pages 60, 61, 64; Pierre Berthiaume: page 82; Richard Burlew: page 49; Leanne Franson: pages 3, 31, 62, 68; Scott Fray: pages 60, 61; Steve Gardner: page 90; Brian Hughes: pages 13, 87; Stephen Hutchings: pages 5, 14, 40, 42, 44: André Labrie: page 72; Andy Meyer: pages 81, 82; Suzanne Mogensen: pages 29, 80, 85; Dušan Petričič: page 22; NSV Productions: pages 30, 33, 39, 41, 58 (top), 86, 87; Joe Sarver: page 46.

ISBN-10: 0-13-392815-2
ISBN-13: 978-0-13-392815-0

Printed in the United States of America
1 2 3 4 5 6 7 8 9 10—V001—19 18 17 16 15 14

pearsonelt.com/topnotch3e

Contents

Getting Acquainted

1   Read about the famous person. Then check <u>true</u>, <u>false</u>, or <u>no information</u>, according to the website.

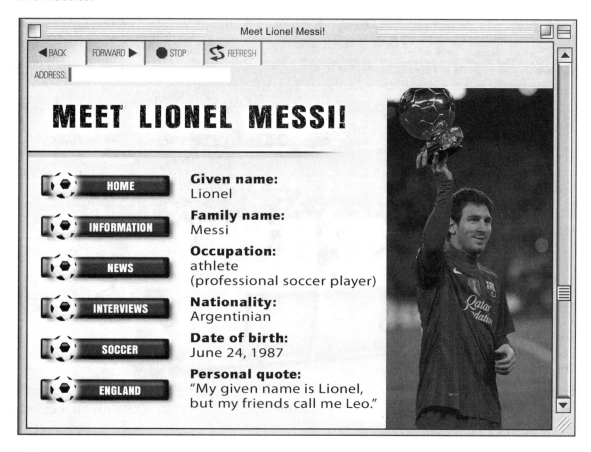

	true	false	no information
1. His first name is Lionel.	☐	☐	☐
2. His last name is Leo.	☐	☐	☐
3. He is an actor.	☐	☐	☐
4. He is married.	☐	☐	☐
5. His nickname is Lionel.	☐	☐	☐

2   Match the word or words with the same meaning. Draw a line.

1. Nice to meet you.   **a.** not married

2. first name   **b.** given name

3. last name   **c.** It's a pleasure to meet you.

4. single   **d.** family name

3 Introduce Lionel Messi. Complete the quote. Use a formal title.

> ❝ I'd like to introduce you to _____
>
> _____ . ❞

4 Complete the information. Write <u>your</u> name on the lines.

HELLO

MY NAME IS _____
         first name   last name

PLEASE CALL ME _____.

Most Common Family Names

Country	Family Name
China	Li
France	Martin
Great Britain	Smith
India	Patel
Japan	Sato
Korea	Kim
Russia	Ivanov
Spain	Garcia
United States	Smith
Vietnam	Nguyen

LESSON 1

5 Choose the correct response. Circle the letter.

1. "Who's that?"
   a. Please call me Matt.   b. Great to meet you.   c. That's my brother, Ryan.

2. "My name's Sidney, and this is Sam."
   a. Hi. I'm Rachel.   b. I think they're new.   c. I'm from Australia.

3. "My name's Elizabeth, but everyone calls me Ellie."
   a. Let's say hello.   b. It's a pleasure to meet you.   c. I'd like you to meet Ellie.

4. "Where are you from?"
   a. London.   b. Twenty-five.   c. A student.

6 Complete the information questions. Use contractions when possible.

1. A: _____ that?
   B: That's Mr. Miller.

2. A: _____ her occupation?
   B: She's an artist.

3. A: Your son is very cute.
   _____ he?
   B: He's eight months old.

4. A: I'll send you an e-mail. _____ your e-mail address?
   B: It's <u>une-yoshiko@videotech.co.jp</u>.

5. A: _____ Anil and Temel from?
   B: They're from Istanbul, I think.

6. A: _____ your new classmates?
   B: That's Marcos on the right and Paulo on the left.

7 Choose the correct response. Write the letter on the line.

_____ 1. "How old is Michael?"

_____ 2. "Who's not here?"

_____ 3. "What are your occupations?"

_____ 4. "Where are their friends from?"

_____ 5. "Where is Ava?"

_____ 6. "What city is he from?"

_____ 7. "Who are your teachers?"

a. She's over there.

b. They're from Germany.

c. He's three.

d. Rachel isn't here.

e. Their names are Mr. Park and Ms. Kim.

f. I'm a singer, and he's a student.

g. He's from Tokyo.

8 Look at the picture. Write a question for each answer.

1. A: _____?

   B: They're my friends from computer class.

2. A: _____?

   B: Their names are Juan and Paloma.

3. A: _____?

   B: Spain.

4. A: _____?

   B: She's two years old.

9 Answer the questions. Use your own words.

1. "Who's your teacher?"

(YOU) _____

2. "What's your e-mail address?"

(YOU) _____

3. "How old are you?"

(YOU) _____

10 Unscramble the words to write sentences.

1. actor / wonderful / is / Suraj Sharma / a

   _____

2. fantastic / a / athlete / is / Lionel Messi

   _____

3. Juan Gabriel Vásquez / writer / is / great / a

   _____

4. are / musicians / The Gipsy Kings / excellent

   _____

5. beautiful / is / Zhang Ziyi / and actress / a / singer

   _____

6. chef / a / Nobu Matsuhisa / famous / is

   _____

11 Look at the responses. Complete the <u>yes</u> / <u>no</u> questions with <u>be</u>.

1. A: _____ Stacey?
   B: No, I'm not. I'm Claire.

2. A: _____ English?
   B: No, they're not. They're Australian.

3. A: _____ a student here?
   B: Yes, he is. I think he's new.

4. A: _____ married?
   B: No, I'm not. I'm single.

5. A: _____ in the same class?
   B: Yes, we are.

6. A: _____ a good chef?
   B: She sure is.

12 Look at the picture. Write short answers about the people.

1. Are Andy and Tara students?

   Yes, they are.

2. Is John an athlete?

   _____

3. Is Maria from Venezuela?

   _____

4. Are Linda and Mike married?

   _____

13 **CHALLENGE.** Write <u>yes</u> / <u>no</u> questions with <u>be</u> about the people from Exercise 10.

1. Suraj Sharma / in the movie *Life of Pi* _____

2. Lionel Messi / a soccer player _____

3. Juan Gabriel Vásquez / a Simón Bolívar Prize winner _____

4. The Gipsy Kings' songs / in French _____

5. Zhang Ziyi / from Hong Kong _____

6. Nobu Matsuhisa / sushi chef _____

Can you answer the questions? Write short answers. Use contractions when possible.
If you don't know, guess.

1. *Yes, he is.* _____ 4. _____

2. _____ 5. _____

3. _____ 6. _____

14 Answer the questions. Use your own words.

1. "Are you a good singer?" **YOU** _____

2. "Are you a good athlete?" **YOU** _____

3. "Are any of your friends or family members famous?" **YOU** _____

LESSONS **3** and **4**

15 Read about where the people are from. Guess their nationalities. Use <u>yes</u> / <u>no</u> questions.

1. A: "My hometown is Vancouver."
   B: _____?

2. A: "I'm from Beijing."
   B: _____?

3. A: "I'm originally from London."
   B: _____?

4. A: "I'm actually from Istanbul."
   B: _____?

16 Answer the questions. Use your own words.

1. "What's your nationality?" **YOU** _____

2. "What's your birthplace?" **YOU** _____

3. "What's your hometown?" **YOU** _____

4. "What's your occupation?" **YOU** _____

5. "What's your nickname?" **YOU** _____

17   Read the letter and reply on an intercultural exchange website.

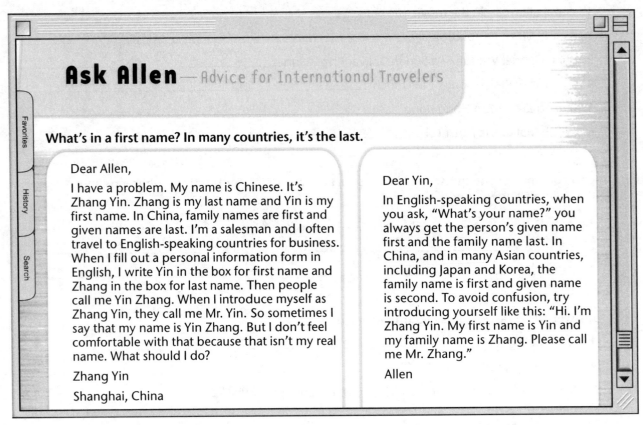

Ask Allen — Advice for International Travelers

Favorites

History

Search

What's in a first name? In many countries, it's the last.

Dear Allen,

I have a problem. My name is Chinese. It's Zhang Yin. Zhang is my last name and Yin is my first name. In China, family names are first and given names are last. I'm a salesman and I often travel to English-speaking countries for business. When I fill out a personal information form in English, I write Yin in the box for first name and Zhang in the box for last name. Then people call me Yin Zhang. When I introduce myself as Zhang Yin, they call me Mr. Yin. So sometimes I say that my name is Yin Zhang. But I don't feel comfortable with that because that isn't my real name. What should I do?

Zhang Yin

Shanghai, China

Dear Yin,

In English-speaking countries, when you ask, "What's your name?" you always get the person's given name first and the family name last. In China, and in many Asian countries, including Japan and Korea, the family name is first and given name is second. To avoid confusion, try introducing yourself like this: "Hi. I'm Zhang Yin. My first name is Yin and my family name is Zhang. Please call me Mr. Zhang."

Allen

Now read the sentences. Check <u>true</u>, <u>false</u>, or <u>no information</u>.

	true	false	no information
1. Zhang Yin's nationality is Chinese.	☐	☐	☐
2. Zhang Yin's family name is Yin.	☐	☐	☐
3. Zhang Yin is a computer programmer.	☐	☐	☐
4. Zhang Yin is married.	☐	☐	☐
5. In China, you say a person's family name first.	☐	☐	☐

18   Read the article "Who Uses English?" on page 10 of the Student's Book again. Answer the questions.

EXTRA READING COMPREHENSION

1. What is Mr. Tanaka's wife's name? What is their son's name?

_____

2. What is Mr. Tanaka's first name?

_____

3. What is the nationality of Ms. Marques' company?

_____

4. How does Ms. Marques use English in her free time?

_____

5. How old is Mr. Itani's son?

_____

6. How does Mr. Itani practice English at home?

_____

19 Read about a famous athlete.

Roger Federer

Name:	Roger Federer
Nickname:	Federer Express
Occupation:	Professional athlete (tennis player)
Date of birth:	August 8, 1981
Nationality:	Swiss
Hometown:	Basel, Switzerland
Now lives in:	Wollerau, Switzerland

Interesting facts: He speaks Swiss-German, English, German, and French (also some Swedish and Italian). He is the father of twin girls born in 2009, and twin boys born in 2014. In his free time, he likes to play video games.

Now write a paragraph introducing Roger Federer. Use the paragraphs on page 11 of the Student's Book as a model.

GRAMMAR BOOSTER

A Look at the responses. Write information questions. Use contractions when possible.

1. A: _What's your name?_

   B: It's Margaret. But my nickname is Maggie.

2. A: _____

   B: My son? He's five.

3. A: _____

   B: I'm from Turkey.

4. A: _____

   B: They are my brothers. Their names are Ishaan and Mahin.

5. A: _____

   B: It's <u>agarcia@ecotech.com</u>. I check my work e-mail every day.

B Add apostrophes (') to the possessive nouns.

1. My <u>parents</u> nationalities? My mom is Korean, and my dad is Irish.

2. Our <u>teachers</u> name is Mr. Springer.

3. <u>Rosas</u> hometown is Recife, in Brazil.

4. The <u>salespersons</u> wife is from Canada. Her English is excellent.

5. Adriana has two boys and a girl. Her <u>sons</u> birthplace is Quito, but her <u>daughters</u> birthplace is New York.

C Complete each sentence with a possessive adjective from the box.

my	your	his	her	our	their

1. Anya and Simon are new students. _____ teacher is Mr. Michaels.

2. Mr. Vidal is a computer programmer. _____ family lives in Paris.

3. Mrs. Ichikawa is from Tokyo. _____ nationality is Japanese.

4. Are you a photographer? _____ pictures are fantastic.

5. I'd like you to meet _____ sister Sarah. She's a musician.

6. Lucy and I are in a computer class. _____ class is at 9 A.M.

D Complete the conversations with words from the box.

they	their	you	your	he	his	she	her	we	our

1. **A:** Who's that?
   B: That's Ajit's brother. _____ name is Raj.
   A: How old is _____?
   B: Twenty-three, I think.

2. **A:** Are _____ the new English teacher?
   B: Yes, I am.
   A: Hi, I'm Chung. What's _____ name?
   B: David Lane. But everyone calls me DJ.

3. **A:** These are my two sons.
   B: What are _____ names?
   A: Jack and Owen.
   B: Are _____ students?
   A: Yes, they are.

4. **A:** Hi, Ha-na.
   B: Hello, Su-ji. Are _____ classmates again?
   A: Yes, I think so. Is that _____ teacher over there?
   B: Yes. _____ name is Mrs. Kim.
   A: _____ looks very young!

E Complete the sentences. Use contractions.

1. You don't know where Liverpool is? _____ in England.

2. My job is wonderful. _____ an interpreter, and I meet people from all over the world.

3. Ms. Kusefoglu's hometown is Konya. _____ Turkish.

4. His name is Mr. Yu. _____ a photographer.

5. Our children are James and Lily. _____ six and four years old.

6. Irina and I are from Moscow. _____ Russian.

7. She lives in São Paulo, but _____ Brazilian. She's from Argentina.

8. Chang is his family name. _____ his given name.

F Answer the <u>yes</u> / <u>no</u> questions with short answers. Answer the information questions with complete sentences. Use contractions when possible.

1. Is Lionel Messi American? _____

2. What is Mr. Messi's occupation? _____

3. Is Mr. Messi's nickname Leo? _____

4. Are you a fan of soccer? _____

5. Where is Roger Federer from? _____

6. Is Mr. Federer a father? _____

7. Are you a tennis player? _____

8. How old are Mr. Messi and Mr. Federer? _____

WRITING BOOSTER

A Look at the personal information. Correct the capitalization.

Name: ᴹmarc anthony

Nickname: skinny

Date of birth: september 16, 1968

Occupation: singer, actor, songwriter

Hometown: new york city

Parents' Birthplace: puerto rico

Favorite music: salsa

Favorite singer: rubén blades

B Rewrite the following paragraph. Use correct capitalization.

mia wasikowska is a famous australian actress. her date of birth is october 14, 1989.
ms. wasikowska's birthplace is canberra, australia. now she lives outside of sydney. she can
speak english with two different accents. this is great for her occupation. ms. wasikowska has
a brother and a sister, kai and jess. her mother is from poland.

C Write a short description of Marc Anthony. Use the information from Exercise A.
Use the paragraph from Exercise B as a guide.

1 Look at the newspaper concert listings. Then complete the chart.

Latin Music Dance Party
Featuring Salsa superstar
Marc Anthony
Show starts at 10:30 P. M. at the Havana Club. Tickets: $35

JAZZ IN THE PARK
An afternoon of jazz with
James Carter
"One of the best jazz saxophonists today!"
(*The New York Times*)
Concert begins at 12:45 P. M. in Riverfront Park. Tickets are $23.

Arcade Fire
ROCK N' ROLL FROM MONTREAL, CANADA
11:30 P. M.
CONTINENTAL CLUB
TICKETS $30

An evening of classical music with world-renowned classical pianist
Alfred Brendel
Beethoven's piano sonatas Nos. 8, 9, and 13. Performance begins at 8:00 P.M. at City Music Hall. Tickets are $60.

Who is playing?	What kind of music?	Where is it?	What time is the show?	How much are tickets?
Marc Anthony	Latin		10:30 P.M.	
James Carter		Riverfront Park		
				$30
	classical	City Music Hall		

2 What's your style? Check <u>Not for me</u> or <u>More my style</u>.

Kind of concert	Not for me	More my style
an afternoon jazz concert in the park	☐	☐
a late night rock concert at a club	☐	☐
a classical concert at a concert hall	☐	☐
live salsa music at a dance club	☐	☐

What's past your bedtime?
Circle the times.
9:30 PM 10:30 PM 11:30 PM
12:30 AM 2:30 AM

3 Complete the paragraph with kinds of music and concert times. Use your own words.

I like _____ music, but _____ music isn't really my style. A concert at _____ is too late for me, but a concert at _____ is perfect.

4 **Choose the correct response. Circle the letter.**

1. "What time's the show?"
   a. At the theater.   b. On Thursday.   c. At 8:30.

2. "I'm busy on Friday. Maybe some other time."
   a. How about Friday?   b. Perfect!   c. Too bad.

3. "Where's the concert?"
   a. In the park.   b. In ten minutes.   c. On August 2nd.

4. "Are you free on Sunday at noon? There's a great exhibit at Gallery Z."
   a. I'd love to go.   b. That's past my bedtime.   c. What time?

5 **Put the conversation in order. Write the number on the line.**

___1___ Are you busy on Saturday night?

_____ 10:00 P.M.? Well, I'd like to go, but that's past my bedtime.

_____ Really? Sounds great! What time's the play?

_____ *Mamma Mia!* is at the Community Theater.

_____ At 10:00 P.M. It's a late show.

_____ No, I'm not. Why?

_____ Too bad. Maybe some other time.

6 **Complete the sentences with <u>on</u>, <u>in</u>, or <u>at</u>.**

1. The movie theater is _____ Dewey Street.

2. The play is _____ noon, _____ the park.

3. Ana isn't here. She's _____ New York.

4. Her class is _____ the Cooper Music School. It's _____ the corner of 2nd and Park.

5. The talk is _____ 11:00 _____ the morning.

6. The Shakira concert is _____ Friday, January 18th.

7. I can't talk right now. I'm _____ work. I'll call you when I get home.

8. Great! I'll meet you in front of the theater _____ twenty minutes.

7 **Write questions with <u>When</u>, <u>Where</u>, or <u>What time</u>. Use contractions when possible.**

1. A: *When's the play* _____? B: The play is on Wednesday.

2. A: _____? B: The concert is at 7:00.

3. A: _____? B: The school is on Saddle Avenue.

4. A: _____? B: Michael's at work.

5. A: _____? B: My class is on Monday morning.

6. A: _____? B: The exhibit is at the Art Center.

7. A: _____? B: The author's talk is at 7:30.

8 Answer the questions. Use your own words. Use <u>in</u>, <u>on</u>, or <u>at</u>.

1. "Where is your school?"

   (YOU) _____

2. "What time is your English class?"

   (YOU) _____

3. "When are you free this week?"

   (YOU) _____

LESSON **2**

9 Choose the correct responses to complete the conversation. Write the letter on the line.

A: Excuse me. I'm looking for Palermo's.

B: _____
    1.

A: Yes. Is it around here?

B: _____
    2.

A: It's 610 Pine Street.

B: _____
    3.

A: Really? That's great. Thanks.

B: _____
    4.

a. Well, Pine Street is right around the corner.

b. I think it is. Do you know the address?

c. No problem.

d. Palermo's? The Italian restaurant?

10 Look at the pictures. Answer the questions.

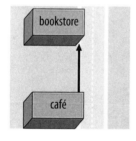

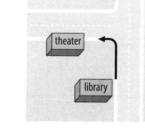

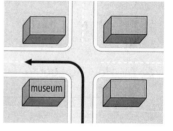

1. Where's the bookstore?

It's down the street from the café.

2. Where's the theater?

3. How do I get to the museum?

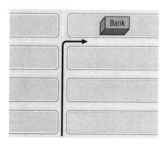

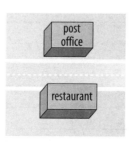

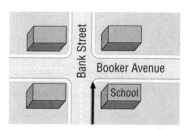

4. How do I get to the bank?

5. Where's the post office?

6. How do I get to the school?

11　Look at the map. Answer the questions.

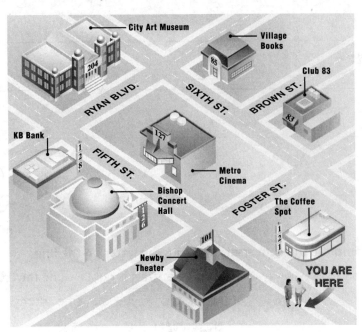

1. **A:** Where's the Metro Cinema?

   B: _____

2. **A:** How do I get to the City Art Museum?

   B: _____

3. **A:** Where's KB Bank?

   B: _____

4. **A:** How do I get to the Newby Theater?

   B: _____

5. **A:** Where's Club 83?

   B: _____

6. **A:** How do I get to Village Books?

   B: _____

12　**CHALLENGE.** Write directions from your home to your school or a place in your community.

Start at: _____ (your address)

Go: _____

_____

_____

_____

_____

_____

End at: _____ (address of final destination)

13 Look at the festival events listing. Then answer the questions. Use <u>in</u>, <u>on</u>, or <u>at</u>, if possible.

10th Annual Asian Folk Festival
Saturday, May 10th at the Park Arts Center in Rand Park
Events Listing

	Time	Location	Event	
	1:00 P.M.	Rand Park	Kite-Making Workshop	Children can make their own kite to fly in the park
	3:00 P.M.	The Park Arts Theater	Japanese Play: Children's Kabuki Group	Watch middle school students from Kobe, Japan perform a traditional play
	7:00 P.M.	The Rand Park Band Shell	Javanese Concert: Kiai Kanjeng Gamelan Orchestra	Hear music featuring drums, cymbals, and gongs from Java, Indonesia
	6:00 P.M.	The Rand Park Band Shell	Korean Dance: "Bu-che Chum" Fan Dance Troupe	See colorful dancers from Suwon, Korea perform a beautiful fan dance
	5:00 P.M. and 9:45 P.M.	The Park Arts Theater	Chinese Movie: *The Story of Lotus*	A love story set in the beautiful Wuyi mountains in Southern China

Plus try traditional Asian treats from China, Japan, Korea, and Indonesia. Food stalls will be open in the park from 12:00 to 8:00 P.M.

1. When's the Asian Folk Festival? _____

2. Where's the Japanese play? _____

3. What time is the Javanese concert? _____

4. Where's the Chinese movie? _____

5. What event is at 6:00 P.M.? _____

14 Complete the instant messages with information from the Asian Folk Festival listing.

```
Lara - Conversation                                              _ □ ☒

File  Edit  Actions  Tools  Help

Invite   Send Files   Webcam   Audio   Launch Site

To: Lara  Lara@email.com
```

Peter says: Hi, Lara. Are you free on [_____] ?
  1.
Lara says: Yes. Why?
Peter says: The Asian Folk Festival is at the [_____], in [_____].
  2.   **3.**
Lara says: What kind of festival?
Peter says: An Asian culture festival. Let's see . . . There's a Chinese movie, a Japanese [_____]
  4.
  a Korean [_____], and a Javanese [_____].
  5.   **6.**
Lara says: Really? Sounds like fun! 😊
Peter says: I know you're a movie fan. Want to see the movie?
Lara says: OK. 👍 What time?
Peter says: There's an early show at [_____] and a late show at 9:45.
  7.
Lara says: Let's go to the early show—9:45 is past my bedtime! 😴

15 Read the interviews on page 22 of the Student's Book again. How would the people here answer questions about their musical tastes? Check all correct answers.

Wayne Seok

Do you go to concerts?
◯ yes   ◯ no

How do you listen to music?
◯ on CDs
◯ on the Internet
◯ on the radio
◯ on music videos
◯ on TV music channels
◯ on my phone

Matheus Rocha

Do you play in a band?
◯ yes   ◯ no

What's your favorite kind of music?
◯ rock / pop
◯ jazz
◯ R&B
◯ Latin
◯ classical
◯ hip-hop

Katherine Baldwin

Are you a music lover?
◯ yes   ◯ no

When do you listen to music?
◯ when I read
◯ when I drive
◯ when I prepare classes
◯ when I eat
◯ when I check e-mail
◯ when I exercise

16 Complete the statements with words from the box, based on information from the interviews on page 22 of the Student's Book.

shows	jazz	computer	genres	MP3s	app

1. Rock, electronic, and hip-hop are Mr. Seok's favorite music _____ .

2. Mr. Seok streams music with an _____ on his smart phone.

3. Mr. Rocha loves American _____ artists.

4. Mr. Rocha listens to music on his phone or his _____ .

5. Ms. Baldwin listens to _____ or online radio.

6. Ms. Baldwin prefers _____ in small clubs.

17 Read about the WOMAD festival. Then check <u>true</u>, <u>false</u>, or <u>no information</u>.

WOMAD festivals celebrate the international language of music.

One of the largest music festivals in the world is WOMAD. WOMAD stands for World of Music, Arts, and Dance. The first WOMAD festival was in 1982, in Somerset, England. Since then, WOMAD has held more than 120 festivals in 21 countries. It has featured over 1,000 musicians, dancers, and artists from 90 different countries. Concert-goers hear rock, jazz, and folk music from all over the world, and go to workshops to learn about the music and instruments they hear.

		true	false	no information
1.	You can see a concert at the WOMAD festival.	☐	☐	☐
2.	WOMAD is a classical music festival.	☐	☐	☐
3.	WOMAD tickets cost $90.	☐	☐	☐
4.	The musicians at WOMAD are from England.	☐	☐	☐

GRAMMAR BOOSTER

A Complete the sentences. Write <u>in</u>, <u>on</u>, or <u>at</u> on the line.

1. There are concerts _____ Saturday afternoons.
2. The bookstore is _____ my neighborhood.
3. My brother lives _____ Rome.
4. The lecture is _____ an art gallery.
5. I finish work _____ two hours.
6. I'm busy _____ the morning.
7. Chile is _____ South America.
8. My house is _____ Carmel Road.
9. The movie is over _____ midnight.
10. My parents got married _____ the 1980s.

B Choose the correct answer. Circle the letter.

1. "Where's the play?"
   a. At The Grand Theater.   b. At 7:30.   c. In the evening.

2. "What time is the movie in the park?"
   a. In March.   b. Tomorrow.   c. At 10:30.

3. "When's the concert?"
   a. On Friday.   b. On Ninth Avenue.   c. At my school.

4. "What time is class?"
   a. In the evening.   b. At 8:15.   c. At the bank.

5. "Where's her meeting?"
   a. On Tuesday.   b. At noon.   c. At 44 South Street.

6. "When's the art exhibit?"
   a. In the center of town.   b. In November.   c. At the City Museum.

7. "What time's the talk?"
   a. September 21.   b. Today.   c. At 1 P.M.

C Complete the event listings with prepositions of time and place. Write <u>in</u>, <u>at</u>, or <u>on</u>.

Arts Week

VOL 1.

Band Plans Free Concert

The Swingtime Jazz Band's first free concert is __at__ 8 P.M. _____
                                                   1.   **2.**
Monday. It's _____ Grand Hall _____ Wakefield Street _____ downtown
             3.   **4.**   **5.**
Wellington. Call 999-555-8443 for more information.

Miracle Worker at Victoria University

Victoria University presents the play *The Miracle Worker* _____
                                                            6.
7:30 P.M. _____ Friday and Saturday, 4/23—4/24, and _____ 2:30 P.M.
          7.   **8.**
_____ April 25. The performances are _____ The Adam Concert Hall
9.   **10.**
_____ Kelburn Road.
11.

D Complete the conversations. Write questions with <u>When</u>, <u>Where</u>, or <u>What time</u>. Complete the responses with a preposition.

1. **A:** _Where's the play_ ?

   B: The play is _at_ The Landry Theater.

2. **A:** _____ ?

   B: I think the concert is _____ 8:30.

3. **A:** _____ ?

   B: The movie theater is _____ Park Road.

4. **A:** _____ ?

   B: The exhibit is _____ January and February.

E Think of an event you'd love to go to. Answer the questions.

1. What's the event?

   (YOU) _____

2. When's the event?

   (YOU) _____

3. What time's the event?

   (YOU) _____

4. Where's the event?

   (YOU) _____

5. Who can you invite?

   (YOU) _____

6. Pretend to invite someone. What do you say?

   (YOU) _____

WRITING BOOSTER

A Circle the subject and underline the verb in each sentence.

1. I love live music at jazz clubs.

2. U2 is a rock band from Dublin, Ireland.

3. Her parents aren't fans of hip-hop music.

4. *Mamma Mia!* is her favorite musical.

5. My husband listens to music on his commute.

6. They download music from the Internet.

7. Salsa music is fun to dance to.

B Look at the music survey on page 23 of the Student's Book. Read the questions.
Write your answers in complete sentences.

1. Are you a music fan?

   YOU _____

2. What's your favorite kind of music?

   YOU _____

3. Who are your favorite singers?

   YOU _____

4. When do you listen to music?

   YOU _____

5. Do you go to concerts?

   YOU _____

6. How do you listen to music?

   YOU _____

7. How many songs are in your library?

   YOU _____

Now circle the subject and underline the verb in each of your sentences. Check that
each sentence begins with a capital letter and ends with a period.

C Look at the music survey on page 23 of the Student's Book. Ask a partner the questions. On a
separate sheet of paper, write at least five sentences about your partner and his / her musical taste.

My partner's name is . . .

UNIT 3 The Extended Family

1 Complete the chart. Use the Vocabulary from page 26 of the Student's Book.

Family relationships		
Words for males	Words for females	Words for males and females
son	daughter	children

2 Complete the sentences with the correct family relationship.

1. My sister's son is my _____ .
2. My mother's parents are my _____ .
3. My mother's brother's son is my _____ .
4. My sister's _____ is my brother-in-law.
5. My brother's daughter is my _____ .
6. My wife's parents are my _____ .

3 **CHALLENGE.** Look at the family tree website. Complete the sentences.

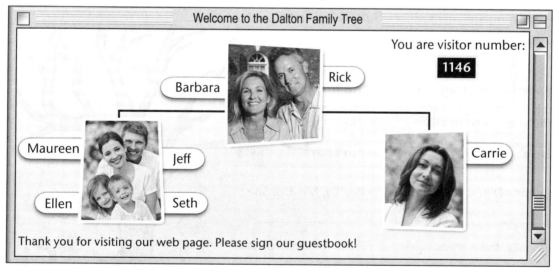

Welcome to the Dalton Family Tree

You are visitor number: **1146**

Barbara   Rick

Maureen   Jeff   Carrie

Ellen   Seth

Thank you for visiting our web page. Please sign our guestbook!

1. Maureen is a <u>daughter-in-law</u>, a <u>wife</u>, a <u>sister-in-law</u>, and a <u>mother</u>.
2. Carrie is a _____, a _____, a _____, and an _____ .
3. Seth is a _____, a _____, a _____, and a _____ .
4. Rick is a _____, a _____, a _____, and a _____ .

4 Complete the sentences. Use words from the box.

twins	adopted	an only child

1. My cousin Karen doesn't have any brothers or sisters. She's _____ .

2. Maddie and her brother Thomas were born on the same day. They're _____ .

3. Jake's mom and dad aren't his birth parents. He's _____ .

LESSON 1

5 Match the words with similar meanings. Write the letter on the line.

_____ 1. divorced   a. married but not living together

_____ 2. single   b. ex-husband and ex-wife

_____ 3. married   c. planning to get married

_____ 4. engaged   d. not married

_____ 5. separated   e. husband and wife

_____ 6. widowed   f. husband or wife is dead

6 Complete the sentences. Use <u>live</u>, <u>have</u>, or <u>work</u> in the simple present tense.

1. She's married. She _____ in an apartment with her husband.

2. He's single. He _____ a wife.

3. My sister is separated. She _____ a husband, but they _____ in the same house.

4. She's engaged to her co-worker. She and her fiancé _____ in the same office.

5. Kevin is divorced. His two children _____ with his wife, but they visit him on weekends.

7 Complete the paragraph. Use words from the box.

likes	doesn't like	works	has
live	work	doesn't have	lives

Juanita Diaz _____ in Puebla, Mexico. She
                    1.
_____ in a restaurant. She _____
    2.   3.
Latin jazz, but she _____ rock music. She's not
                          4.
really a rock fan. She _____ any children, but
                            5.
she _____ two nieces and one nephew. They
         6.
_____ in Tampico with Juanita's sister, Maria.
      7.
Maria and her husband Roberto _____ in a
                                        8.
school. They are both teachers.

8 Write <u>yes</u> / <u>no</u> questions and give short answers.

1. A: <u>Do they live in New York?</u>
   B: <u>Yes, they do.</u>
   (They live in New York.)

2. A: _____
   B: _____
   (Mr. Kelly has a large family.)

3. A: _____
   B: _____
   (They don't work in my building.)

4. A: _____
   B: _____
   (I speak English at work.)

5. A: _____
   B: _____
   (She lives with her parents.)

6. A: _____
   B: _____
   (We don't have any children.)

7. A: _____
   B: _____
   (My husband doesn't like show tunes.)

8. A: _____
   B: _____
   (I don't live with my sister.)

9 Choose the correct response to complete the conversation. Write the letter on the line.

A: _____
       1.
B: Actually, I have some good news and some bad news.

A: _____
       2.
B: My niece just got married.

A: _____
       3.
B: Thanks!

A: _____
       4.
B: My brother and sister-in-law just got separated.

A: _____
       5.

a. Really? That's fantastic.

b. What's new?

c. What's the good news?

d. Oh, no. I'm sorry to hear that.

e. What's the bad news?

10 Answer the questions. Use your own words.

1. "Do you live near your parents?"
   (YOU) _____

2. "Do you have any nieces or nephews?"
   (YOU) _____

3. "Do you work? What do you do?"
   (YOU) _____

LESSON 2

11 Read the information. Complete the statements.

> Hi. My name is Brianna. My parents got divorced when I was very young. After a few years, my mother got married again. Her second husband's name is Ray. They have a daughter, Gabby. Gabby and I grew up together and we're very close. My father just got remarried. His new wife, Katherine, has two young boys, Jess and Avery. It's fun having two little brothers. They live nearby, so sometimes I baby-sit for them.

1. Brianna is Ray's _____ .

2. Gabby is Brianna's _____ .

3. Katherine is Brianna's _____ .

4. Brianna is Jess and Avery's _____ .

5. Brianna's father is Jess and Avery's _____ .

12 Complete the questions with <u>do</u> or <u>does</u>.

1. Where _____ Aidan live?

2. When _____ you listen to music?

3. What _____ your half-brother do?

4. How often _____ you go to the movies?

5. What time _____ your husband go to work?

6. What _____ your friends call you?

7. How many brothers and sisters _____ you have?

13 Choose the correct response. Write the letter on the line.

_____ 1. "What does Alex do?"

_____ 2. "How many children does your sister have?"

_____ 3. "Where does your mother live?"

_____ 4. "How often do you call your stepsister?"

_____ 5. "What time do you get home from work?"

_____ 6. "When do you visit your grandmother?"

_____ 7. "What do you and your husband do?"

a. In Madrid with my half-sister.

b. At 6:30.

c. He works at a bookstore.

d. We talk on the phone every day.

e. She has three.

f. On Sunday afternoons.

g. We're both teachers.

14 Look at the responses. Complete the questions.

1. A: ___What does___ Nick ___do___ ?

   B: He's a computer programmer.

2. A: _____ your cousins _____ ?

   B: They live in Hong Kong.

3. A: _____ your mother _____ you?

   B: She visits me every year in May.

4. A: _____ concert tickets _____ ?

   B: I only have two.

5. A: _____ to school?

   B: We go at 8:30.

6. A: _____ a twin brother or sister?

   B: My friend Allison has a twin sister. Her name is Emma.

15 Write a paragraph about someone in your family. Use these questions for ideas.

- Who is it? What's his or her relationship to you?
- Where does he or she live?
- What does he or she do?
- Is he or she married or single?
- How many children (or brothers and sisters) does he or she have?
- How often / When do you see him or her?

16 Complete the sentences. Use words from the box.

same	kind	different	both	alike	but

1. Robert and Peter wear dark suits to work. They wear the same _____ of clothes.

2. Megan eats salads for lunch. Frank eats cheeseburgers and french fries. They like _____ foods.

3. Elizabeth and her sister are identical twins. They look exactly _____.

4. Mike likes classical music, _____ Dave listens to rock and hip-hop.

5. My stepsister and I like the same music. We _____ download show tunes and movie soundtracks.

6. Joe and Ryan both eat at this restaurant a lot. They like the _____ kind of food.

17 Look at the pictures. Complete the sentences.

Mary   Ida   Miki   Jamie

1. Mary and Ida _____ wear glasses.   2. Miki is a chef, _____ Jamie isn't.

Do you speak English?

Antonio   Yoko   Jim   Thomas

3. Antonio speaks English, but Yoko _____.   4. Jim is a jazz fan, but Thomas _____.

18 Look at the questions and answers. Write sentences comparing the two people.

	Jane	Mark
Do you like rock concerts?	yes	no
Do you have an MP3 player?	yes	yes

1. Jane likes rock concerts, but Mark doesn't.
2. Jane and Mark both have MP3 players.

	Chris	Lola
Do you like coffee?	yes	yes
Do you eat a big breakfast?	yes	no

3. _____
4. _____

	Mia	Rose
Do you have a large family?	yes	no
Do you live near your parents?	no	yes

5. _____
6. _____

	Joon	Sam
Are you a student?	yes	no
Do you work?	yes	yes

7. _____
8. _____

19 Choose four relatives. Write each person's name, relationship to you, and one similarity or difference.

1. Name: _____ Relationship: _____
   Similarity / Difference: _____
   (Circle one.)

2. Name: _____ Relationship: _____
   Similarity / Difference: _____
   (Circle one.)

3. Name: _____ Relationship: _____
   Similarity / Difference: _____
   (Circle one.)

4. Name: _____ Relationship: _____
   Similarity / Difference: _____
   (Circle one.)

20 Read the family advice column.

Ask Dr. Neaman: Advice for Families

Dear Dr. Neaman,

I just got engaged to a wonderful man. My fiancé, Jim, is widowed. He has two children from his first marriage. His son is eight and his daughter is five. I am divorced. I have one child—a three-year-old son—from my first marriage. I'm excited about my new family, but I'm a little worried, too. I know that relationships between stepparents and stepchildren can be difficult. What can I do to make sure my new blended family is happy together?

Eleanor D.

Mesa, Arizona

Hi, Eleanor,

First of all, congratulations on your engagement! There is one thing you should know—you are not alone. Blended families—in which at least one parent has a child from another relationship—are very common in the U.S. More than 65% of Americans belong to a blended family. In fact, there are 2,100 new blended families every day.

You are correct—starting a blended family can be difficult. Getting married is exciting for the parents. But children may feel unhappy about sharing their birth parent's love and attention. They may worry about their new family members. Will they have a good relationship with their new stepfather or stepmother? What will their new stepbrothers and stepsisters be like? Moving to a new home and school is also stressful. With more people living together, children may have less personal space.

The good news is that many blended families learn to love each other. The bad news? Creating a happy family takes hard work and a lot of time. Here are three important tips for new stepparents:

- Be realistic: Everything won't be perfect in the beginning. Expect that there will be some problems.
- Be patient: It may take years for a good relationship to develop. Give the children the time they need.
- Don't expect too much: Give your stepchildren your time, energy, and love, but don't expect anything in return for now.

Good luck!

Dr. Neaman

**Dr. Gabrielle Neaman, Ph.D.
Family Counselor**

Now read the sentences. Check <u>true</u> or <u>false</u>.

		true	false
1.	Jim and his ex-wife are divorced.	☐	☐
2.	Eleanor and Jim have a son.	☐	☐
3.	In a blended family, at least one parent has a child from another relationship.	☐	☐
4.	About 2,100 people in the U.S. live in blended families.	☐	☐
5.	Children in a new blended family may feel worried about moving to a new home or school.	☐	☐
6.	Eleanor may need a long time to develop a strong relationship with her stepchildren.	☐	☐

21 Look at the website on page 34 of the Student's Book again. What advice does "Mr. Dad" offer to worried parents of adult children living at home? Write <u>Do</u> or <u>Don't</u> on the line.

_____ 1. Worry.

_____ 2. Help in any way you can.

_____ 3. Ask, "How long do you plan on staying?"

_____ 4. Treat your adult children like kids.

_____ 5. Tell them you understand.

_____ 6. Talk to them as adults.

_____ 7. Discuss paying for expenses and helping with chores.

GRAMMAR BOOSTER

A Choose the correct response. Write the letter on the line.

_____ 1. "Do you and your brothers play soccer together?"

_____ 2. "Does your stepbrother work in a restaurant?"

_____ 3. "Do your grandparents like music?"

_____ 4. "Does your aunt look like your mother?"

_____ 5. "Do you live near here?"

_____ 6. "Do I need a tie?"

a. No, he doesn't.

b. Yes, we do. All the time.

c. No, I don't.

d. Yes, they do. Very much.

e. No, she doesn't.

f. No, you don't.

B Complete the conversations. Write short answers to the questions.

1. **A:** Does he live in Sydney?

   B: _No, he doesn't_____ . He lives in Melbourne.

2. **A:** Do your friends like Chinese food?

   B: _____ . They go to Chinese restaurants all the time.

3. **A:** Do you have a big family?

   B: _____ . I have eight brothers and sisters.

4. **A:** Does your husband work in an office?

   B: _____ . He's a musician.

5. **A:** Do we need to buy our tickets now?

   B: _____ . We can buy our tickets on the train.

C Complete the conversations. Write <u>yes</u> / <u>no</u> questions with the simple present tense.

1. **A:** He doesn't like concerts.

   B: _Does he like_____ art exhibits?

2. **A:** My sister-in-law doesn't eat meat.

   B: _____ fish?

3. **A:** My stepfather doesn't drink coffee.

   B: _____ tea?

4. **A:** I don't like rock music.

   B: _____ jazz?

5. **A:** I have two brothers and one sister.

   B: _____ any nieces and nephews?

D Look at the responses. Write information questions with the simple present tense.

1. A: _How many people do you have in your office_ ?

   B: In my office? About twenty or twenty-five people.

2. A: _____?

   B: Max? He works in London.

3. A: _____?

   B: They usually start work at 8:00.

4. A: _____?

   B: My mother. She calls me every night.

5. A: _____?

   B: The Perez family lives here.

6. A: _____?

   B: Mona? She only has one sister.

7. A: _____?

   B: He sees his cousins every summer.

E Read each statement. Underline the subject and circle the object. Write two questions with <u>who</u>, one about the subject and one about the object.

1. <u>My son</u> visits (my parents) once a month.

   a. _Who visits your parents once a month_ ? My son.

   b. _Who does your son visit once a month_ ? My parents.

2. My grandmother lives with my aunt.

   a. _____? My grandmother.

   b. _____? My aunt.

3. Nathaniel loves Beethoven.

   a. _____? Nathaniel.

   b. _____? Beethoven.

4. Elliot works for Mr. Kim.

   a. _____? Elliot.

   b. _____? Mr. Kim.

How many people are
there in the world? You can see
a population clock on this website:
www.census.gov/cgi-bin/ipc/popclockw

A Look at the sports website. Complete each sentence with **and** or **but**.

1. Victor Oladipo is tall, _____ he's a basketball player.

2. Victor Oladipo is an athlete, _____ he's a singer.

3. Mr. Duncan has two sisters, _____ Mr. Oladipo has three sisters.

4. Mr. Oladipo likes R&B music, _____ Mr. Duncan doesn't.

5. Mr. Oladipo _____ Mr. Duncan are single now.

6. Mr. Oladipo was born in the 90s, _____ Mr. Duncan was born in the 70s.

B Look at the sports website again. On a separate sheet of paper, write a paragraph comparing Victor Oladipo and Tim Duncan. Write about how they are similar and how they are different.

1 Look at the menus. Then read the conversations. Where are the customers eating? Write the name of the restaurant on the line.

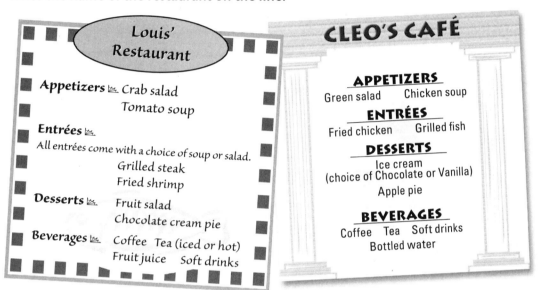

Louis' Restaurant

Appetizers Crab salad
Tomato soup

Entrées
All entrées come with a choice of soup or salad.
Grilled steak
Fried shrimp

Desserts Fruit salad
Chocolate cream pie

Beverages Coffee Tea (iced or hot)
Fruit juice Soft drinks

CLEO'S CAFÉ

APPETIZERS
Green salad Chicken soup

ENTRÉES
Fried chicken Grilled fish

DESSERTS
Ice cream
(choice of Chocolate or Vanilla)
Apple pie

BEVERAGES
Coffee Tea Soft drinks
Bottled water

Are you ready to order?

Yes, thanks. I'll have the fried chicken.

1. _Cleo's Café_

Would you like to start with an appetizer?

Yes, I'd like a green salad.

2. _____

What comes with the entrées?

You have a choice of soup or salad.

3. _____

Anything to drink?

Fruit juice, please.

4. _____

2 Look at the menus in Exercise 1 again. Where will you eat? What food will you order?

I'll eat at _____ . I'll start with the _____ .
Then I'll have the _____ . I'd like _____ to drink
and _____ for dessert.

Now change your mind about one dish your ordered.

On second thought, maybe I'll have the _____ for _____ .

3 Complete the word webs. Write food categories and foods on the lines.

apples
fruits
①

peppers
vegetables
②

oils
corn oil
③

beef
lamb
④

yogurt
dairy products
⑤

cookies   cake
⑥

clams
squid
⑦

pasta
grains
⑧

4 What's in the fridge? Look at the picture. Write sentences starting with <u>There is</u> / <u>There isn't</u> or <u>There are</u> / <u>There aren't</u>.

Non-count nouns	
fish	lettuce
sausage	juice
milk	broccoli
cheese	yogurt

Count nouns	
apple	carrot
banana	orange
egg	onion
grape	

5 Think about your favorite dish at your favorite restaurant. What are the ingredients? Use <u>There is</u> / <u>There are</u> to write the ingredients you know. Use <u>Is there</u> / <u>Are there</u> to guess other ingredients.

Dish: Pad Thai   Restaurant: Lemon Grass
Location: on the corner of First Avenue and Bank Street
There's shrimp in the Pad Thai at Lemon Grass. Are there eggs?

Dish: Restaurant:
Location:

6 Answer the questions. Use your own words.

1. "Is there anything to eat in your fridge?"
   YOU _____

2. "How hungry are you right now?"
   YOU _____

3. "What restaurants in your area do you recommend?"
   YOU _____

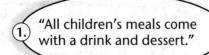

7 **Match the statement on the left with the explanation on the right. Draw a line.**

1. "All children's meals come with a drink and dessert."

a. The customer is asking about the menu.

b. The server is explaining the menu.

2. "Does the grilled chicken come with a salad?"

c. The customer is not ready to order.

d. The server is taking a beverage order.

3. "I think I'll start with the tomato soup."

e. The customer is ordering an appetizer.

f. The server is taking the customer's entrée order.

4. "Anything to drink?"

5. "I need some more time."

The first real restaurant with a menu with a choice of meals opened in 1765 in Paris.

6. "And what would you like for your main course?"

8 **Complete the conversations.**

1. **A:** What do sandwiches _____?
   B: Potato chips or fresh fruit.

2. **A:** What _____ bread is there?
   B: White, wheat, or a croissant.

3. **A:** And anything _____?
   B: Sparkling water, please.

4. **A:** Would you like to try our famous chocolate cake?
   B: No, thanks. I'm not in the _____ dessert.

9 Complete the conversation with **a**, **an**, or **the**.

Mary: Let's get _____ table.
　　　　　　　　　1.

Joan: OK. Let's see. How about _____ table
　　　　　　　　　　　　　　　　　2.
　　　by the window? It's available.

Mary: Perfect.

Server: Are you ready to order?

Joan: Yes, we are. Do you have _____
　　　　　　　　　　　　　　　　3.
　　　breakfast special?

Server: Yes, we do. We have _____ Continental
　　　　　　　　　　　　　　　　4.
　　　Breakfast Special and _____ English
　　　　　　　　　　　　　　5.
　　　Breakfast Special on _____ menu today.
　　　　　　　　　　　　　6.

Joan: What does _____ Continental Breakfast
　　　　　　　　　　　7.
　　　Special come with?

Server: It comes with _____ choice of juice, tea,
　　　　　　　　　　　　8.
　　　or coffee and _____ basket of fresh-baked
　　　　　　　　　　9.
　　　French bread.

Joan: I think I'll have _____ English
　　　　　　　　　　　　10.
　　　Breakfast Special with coffee, please.

Mary: I'll have the same, but without _____ coffee.
　　　　　　　　　　　　　　　　　11.
　　　I'll have _____ glass of juice instead.
　　　　　　　12.

Server: Certainly.

The Sunrise Café

Breakfast Specials:
All specials include your choice of coffee, tea, or juice.

Continental Breakfast:
Basket of fresh-baked French bread

English Breakfast:
Fried Eggs, Sausage, Tomatoes, Fried Potatoes

---

10 Complete the sentences with **a**, **an**, or **the**.

1. I'm in the mood for _____ cheeseburger.

2. _____ Caesar salad at Mario's is fantastic.

3. Is there _____ children's menu?

4. Would you like to start with _____ appetizer?

5. It's Elizabeth's birthday. Let's pick up _____ cake.

6. I recommend _____ curry chicken. It's delicious.

7. Are there eggs in _____ Chinese noodles?

8. For breakfast, I usually have coffee with milk and _____ banana.

9. _____ orange juice here is fresh-squeezed.

---

11 Answer the questions. Use your own words. Use **a**, **an**, or **the** if needed.

1. "Hungry? What are you in the mood for?"
　　YOU _____

2. "What dish do you recommend at your favorite restaurant?"
　　YOU _____

3. "What do you usually eat for breakfast?"
　　YOU _____

12   **Look at the menu. Then answer the questions with short answers.**

1. Does the pasta come with a salad?
    Yes, it does.

2. What kind of soup is there?
    _____

3. Is there any seafood on the menu?
    _____

4. Are there any healthy foods on the menu?
    _____

5. Is the fish entrée spicy?
    _____

6. Does this restaurant accept credit cards?
    _____

7. What kind of salad is there?
    _____

JACK'S RESTAURANT

SOUPS
Clam Chowder   Chicken Vegetable

SALADS
Pasta Salad   Mixed Green Salad

ENTRÉES
ALL ENTRÉES INCLUDE A CHOICE OF SOUP OR SALAD.
Teriyaki Steak with mashed potatoes
Vegetable Beef Stew with carrots, potatoes, and peas
Pasta with tomato sauce
Grilled Fish with garlic and red pepper sauce

LITE ENTRÉES
Low-Fat Baked Chicken with cottage cheese and fresh fruit
Vegetable Sandwich—sweet bell peppers, cucumbers, carrots,
and mixed salad greens on pita bread

BEVERAGES
Bottled Water   Soft Drinks   Tea   Coffee

= This is a hot dish!

SORRY, WE DO NOT ACCEPT CREDIT CARDS.

13   **Read the webpage on page 46 of the Student's Book again. Circle the healthier fast-food options.**

1. **a.** chicken   **b.** red meat
2. **a.** grilled   **b.** fried
3. **a.** food with breading   **b.** food without breading
4. **a.** regular-size portion   **b.** super-size portion
5. **a.** french fries   **b.** fruit cup or side salad
6. **a.** frozen yogurt or fruit ices   **b.** ice cream or cookies

Now answer the questions, according to the website.

1. What's unhealthy about breading?
    _____

2. Why is it a good idea to eat slowly?
    _____

3. What's unhealthy about french fries?
    _____

4. What's healthy about frozen yogurt or fruit ices?
    _____

What will you order the next time you have fast food? Explain why.

14 Create a menu for the Healthy Choice Café. Write healthful foods that you like
to eat under each menu category.

Healthy Choice Café

"Eat out with us and eat smart!"

Appetizers

Raw veggie platter

Soups

Entrées

Desserts

Beverages

GRAMMAR BOOSTER

A Complete the chart with nouns from the box.

| music | apple | water | fun | banana | cheese | help | egg |
| cookie | carrot | sugar | fruit | bread | golf | onion | coffee |

COUNT	NON-COUNT
apple	music

B Write <u>How much</u> or <u>How many</u> to complete the questions. Then answer each question, using a countable quantity. Use your own words.

1. "_____ water do you drink in a day?"

   YOU _____

2. "_____ milk is in your refrigerator?"

   YOU _____

3. "_____ potato chips do you eat in a week?"

   YOU _____

4. "_____ bread do you buy every week?"

   YOU _____

5. "_____ onions do you use in a month?"

   YOU _____

6. "_____ sugar do you put in your coffee?"

   YOU _____

C Complete the e-mail. Write <u>a</u> or <u>an</u> in front of count nouns or <u>x</u> in front of non-count nouns.

Brad,

    I need _____ help with dinner today. Can you go to the store and
              1.

buy _____ liter of milk and _____ loaf of bread? We also need _____ onion
    2.   3.   4.

or two, and _____ kilo of apples. Do you think we have _____ cheese?
           5.   6.

If not, please get _____ package of that, too. I'll see you at home
               7.

after 5:00.

Tracy

D Complete the conversations with <u>some</u> or <u>any</u>. For some items, more than one answer may be possible.

1. **A:** Do you need _____ bread?

   B: No, thanks. I have _____.

2. **A:** Do they want _____ soup?

   B: No, they don't want _____ right now.

3. **A:** I don't have _____ water, and I'm so thirsty.

   B: Do you want _____ tea?

4. **A:** Does she need _____ help?

   B: She doesn't need _____ help. She needs _____ practice.

A Connect the following words and ideas with <u>and</u> and <u>in addition</u>.

1. Spanish paella is made with rice, seafood, meat, _____ vegetables.

2. A traditional Irish breakfast includes sausage, bacon, _____ fried eggs. _____, there are fried potatoes and tomatoes.

3. Pho is a soup from North Vietnam, _____ it's made with beef and rice noodles.

4. Guacamole is a Mexican appetizer made from avocadoes. _____ , it contains tomatoes, onions, lemon or lime juice, _____ salt.

5. Indian samosas are fried pastries, _____ they have a spicy filling of potatoes, peas, onions, _____ green chilis.

B Think of a typical dish from your country. Answer the questions.

1. What is the name of the dish? _____

2. What kind of dish is it (appetizer, entrée, side, etc.)? _____

3. What region of your country is it from? _____

4. What are the main ingredients? _____

5. Is it spicy, salty, or sweet? _____

6. Is it healthy? Why or why not? _____

C Write a paragraph describing the dish from Exercise B. Use <u>and</u> and <u>in addition</u> when possible.

1 Look at the electronics on page 50 of the Student's Book. List the products in each category. Some products can be listed in more than one category.

For listening to music	For watching movies	With your computer
headphones		
While driving	**While on vacation**	

2 Complete the chart. Use electronic products from page 50 of the Student's Book.

Products I have	Products I need / want	Products I can live without

3 Now look at the <u>Products I have</u> column. Choose five products you listed and write them in the chart below. Explain why these products are necessary to you. Use the vocabulary and language from pages 50–51 of the Student's Book.

	Products	Why necessary?
1.	laptop	I use it at work and at home . . .
2.		
3.		
4.		
5.		

4 **Choose the correct response. Circle the letter.**

1. "I'm looking for a new cell phone. Do you have any suggestions?"
   a. What's wrong with it?　　b. Want to come along?　　c. How about a Global Mobile?

2. "What are you doing?"
   a. I'm looking for a camcorder.　b. I'm ready for an upgrade.　c. It's driving me crazy!

3. "I hear the new X-phone is awesome."
   a. Is it on the blink?　　b. Is it expensive?　　c. Is it a lemon?

4. "The photocopier isn't working."
   a. Are you online?　　b. Any suggestions?　　c. What's the problem?

5 **Complete each conversation with the present continuous. Use contractions when possible.**

What _is George doing_ here?
1. George / do

I think _____
2. he / look
for a new TV.

_____ to your
3. you / go
sister's house tonight?

Yes, _____ at 7:00.
4. I / leave

_____ your e-mail?
5. you / check

No, _____ . Mike's Photo
6. I / shop
_____ a sale on digital
7. have
cameras.

Who _____
8. use
the photocopier?

Erin is.
_____ copies for the
9. she / make
sales meeting.

6 Read the questions. Write answers starting with <u>No</u>. Use the information in parentheses. Use contractions when possible.

    1. Is he leaving at 10:30? (11:00)

    No, he isn't. He's leaving at 11:00.

    2. Are they studying at the library? (look at the newspaper ads)

    _____

    3. Are you shopping for a laptop? (a smart phone)

    _____

    4. Is she going to the movie tonight? (tomorrow night)

    _____

7 Write questions starting with <u>Is</u> or <u>Are</u>.

    1. you / look for / a new tablet

    Are you looking for a new tablet?

    2. he / check / e-mail / right now

    _____

    3. they / buy / a scanner

    _____

    4. Kate / work / today

    _____

8 Look at the responses. Complete the questions. Use the present continuous.

    1. **A:** What *are you looking for* ?
        B: I'm looking for a dictionary.

    2. **A:** Who _____?
        B: Matt is going to the tech conference.

    3. **A:** What _____?
        B: I'm buying a new cell phone.

    4. **A:** When _____?
        B: My sister is going to Dublin in September.

9 Look at Maria's smart phone. Answer the questions about her schedule. Use the present continuous. Use contractions when possible.

    1. It's 12:15 P.M. What is Maria doing?

    _____

    2. It's 4:00 P.M. Is Maria going shopping?

    _____

    What is she looking for?

    _____

    3. It's 9:15 P.M. Is Maria eating dinner?

    _____

    What is she doing?

    _____

10:00 A.M.
    Call travel office

11:30 A.M.
    Call Ed about movie

12:00 P.M.
    Have lunch with Peter

4:00 P.M.
    Shopping: Look for webcam

7:00–8:30 P.M.
    Have dinner with Mom and Dad

9:00 P.M.
    See movie with Ed

10 **Answer the questions. Use your own words.**

   1. "Are you using any electronic devices right now?"

   YOU _____

   2. "What are you doing tonight?"

   YOU _____

   3. "What about next weekend?"

   YOU _____

LESSON 2

11 **Complete the conversation. Use questions from the box.**

What's wrong with it?	How's it going?	Any suggestions?	What brand is it?

A: Hi, Barry. _____
                              1.

B: OK, thanks. But my coffee maker's driving me crazy!

A: Not again! _____
                              2.

B: I don't know. It just isn't working. That thing is a piece of junk!

A: That's too bad. _____
                              3.

B: It's a Coffee Pal.

A: Sounds like you need a new coffee maker.

B: That's for sure. _____
                              4.

A: Well, how about a Brewtech? The model I have is terrific.

B: Really? Thanks for the suggestion.

12 **Complete the responses. Use words from the box.**

hair dryer	blender	freezer	washing machine	fan	microwave

   1. A: The juicer isn't working.

   B: Try the _____ .

   2. A: The chicken is still not done. This oven is so slow!

   B: Let's put it in the _____ .

   3. A: Are you ready to go to the Laundromat?

   B: Again? Too much trouble. I hear Appliance World is having a sale on _____s .

   4. A: The air conditioner is on the blink again.

   B: Do we have a _____ ?

   5. A: You look different.

   B: I look horrible! My _____ is broken! I'm going shopping for a new one at lunch.

   6. A: Are we having these steaks tonight?

   B: No, they're for next week. Please put them in the _____ .

13 Write each response in a different way.

1. **A:** What's wrong?
   B: My printer won't print.
   My printer's not working.

2. **A:** What do you think about Pell brand computers?
   B: Pell computers are great!
   _____

3. **A:** My TV isn't working. I can't watch the big game tonight.
   B: I'm sorry to hear that.
   _____

4. **A:** How's your new laptop?
   B: It's a piece of junk!
   _____

14 Answer the questions. Use your own words.

1. "Are you using any household appliances or machines right now?"
   YOU _____

2. "What household appliances and machines do you use every day?"
   YOU _____

3. "What household appliances and machines do you never use? Why?"
   YOU _____

LESSONS 3 and 4

15 Look at the picture. Then complete the paragraph. Use the present continuous.

It's a busy Monday morning at the office of Techco Inc. The company president, Ms. Cline,

_____*is answering*_____ her e-mail. She _____ tomorrow morning. She _____
     1. answer   2. leave   3. go

to Brazil for a sales meeting. Her assistant, Frank, _____ some documents right
                                                     4. scan

now, and he _____ Ms. Cline's airplane tickets online. Jim, a sales manager,
                    5. buy

_____ the photocopier and the fax machine / printer. He _____ copies
     6. use   7. make

of a report for the meeting and _____ a fax to Ms. Cline's hotel. Jeff and Aliza also
                                   8. send

work for Techco. They _____ the break room and _____ coffee.
                       9. clean   10. make

16 Look at the picture. Find all of the problems in the office. Write a short paragraph about the problems.

The employees at Techno are having problems . . .

17 Think about the features of products you have or know about. Write one product for each adjective. Explain your answers.

1. guaranteed: <u>blender</u>
   <u>I can return it if I don't like it.</u>

4. obsolete: _____
   _____

2. portable: _____
   _____

5. popular: _____
   _____

3. affordable: _____
   _____

6. convenient: _____
   _____

18 Read the advertisement on page 58 of the Student's Book again. Then check true, false, or no information.

	true	false	no information
1. The Pro Musica comes with 5 pairs of earbuds.	☐	☐	☐
2. With the Pro Musica, you don't need a radio.	☐	☐	☐
3. Family members can listen to different music at the same time.	☐	☐	☐
4. The Pro Musica comes with its own battery pack.	☐	☐	☐
5. You have to plug the speakers into the Pro Musica.	☐	☐	☐
6. It's easy to download music onto the Pro Musica.	☐	☐	☐

Presenting The Easy Shopper

Do you love to cook but hate to shop? How much time do you spend every day in the supermarket? How many ingredients do you forget to buy? Well, now you can simplify shopping with The Easy Shopper app for your phone.

To use The Easy Shopper, you simply enter the name of the dishes you want to cook into your phone, and we do the hard work. You can choose a big dinner with appetizers, entrées, desserts, and beverages. Or if you're not very hungry, make a smaller meal just for you—maybe a delicious salad or sandwich. The Easy Shopper figures out what ingredients you need to cook this meal and sends the information to a supermarket. The app then gives you two or three different recipes for each dish. The supermarket collects and boxes your ingredients, and your groceries are waiting for you in only ONE HOUR. Finally, you go home and use Easy Shopper's recipes to cook your meal!

No more waiting in supermarket checkout lines. All you have to do is go to an Easy Shopper pick-up location at your supermarket, and we put all your groceries in your car. Just enter the following information in The Easy Shopper:

• What do you feel like eating tonight? Are you in the mood for seafood? Beef? Noodles?

• How hungry are you? Are you starving? Or just a little hungry?
• How many people are you cooking for?
• Are you on any special diet—low-salt or low-fat, for example?

The Easy Shopper costs only $29.99 a month, and we accept all major credit cards. You save both time and money with The Easy Shopper. No more buying ingredients that you never use or spending hours in the supermarket. And if there's a mistake in your order, it's free—yes, FREE! We promise 100% satisfaction!

Hundreds of people are signing up for The Easy Shopper! Ask your friends and neighbors! They'll tell you how great it is. Don't spend another boring evening waiting in line at the supermarket. Get The Easy Shopper today!

Now read the article again. According to the information in the article, which adjectives describe The Easy Shopper? For the adjectives you check, find words in the text to support your answers.

☑ convenient _groceries are waiting for you in one hour; no more waiting in lines_

☐ guaranteed _____

☐ affordable _____

☐ portable _____

☐ popular _____

Do you think that The Easy Shopper is a good app? Would you buy The Easy Shopper today? Explain your answers.

GRAMMAR BOOSTER

A **Change each statement from the simple present tense to the present continuous. Use contractions.**

1. I eat breakfast every morning. *I'm eating breakfast* _____ now.

2. My mother buys a newspaper every day. _____ now.

3. They walk to school every day. _____ now.

4. It rains all the time in the summer. _____ now.

5. He runs in the park every afternoon. _____ now.

6. We close the store at 5 P.M. _____ now.

7. He writes the report on Fridays. _____ now.

B **Write negative statements. Use the words in parentheses.**

1. He's going to school now. *He's not working* _____ . (work)

2. Sonia and Leo are drinking water. _____ . (tea)

3. Ted is writing a letter. _____ . (do homework)

4. You're talking a lot. _____ . (listen)

5. I'm reading a magazine. _____ . (a book)

6. We're eating at my house. _____ . (a restaurant)

7. The printer is making a noise. _____ . (print)

C Choose the correct response. Write the letter on the line.

_____ 1. "Are you going to work now?"   a. A new rice cooker.

_____ 2. "Is he studying for an English test?"   b. No, he's not.

_____ 3. "What is Tina shopping for?"   c. Yes, I am.

_____ 4. "Are they listening to jazz?"   d. In an hour.

_____ 5. "When is he leaving work?"   e. Yuko and Miyumi.

_____ 6. "Who's watching TV?"   f. No, they aren't. It's folk.

D Unscramble the words to write questions. Use the present continuous.

1. go / to the store / who <u>Who is going to the store?</u> _____

2. they / play soccer / where _____

3. Sam / eat / what _____

4. when / Lidia / come home _____

5. my computer / why / use / you _____

6. pay for / you / that / how much / laptop _____

WRITING BOOSTER

A Rewrite the sentences. Use a form of <u>have</u>. Place the adjective before the noun.

1. My GPS is new. <u>I have a new GPS.</u> _____

2. My food processor is convenient. _____

3. Our desktop computer is obsolete. _____

4. Her smart phone is awesome. _____

5. Their laptop is fast. _____

6. His speakers are portable. _____

B Write one sentence. Connect the adjectives with <u>and</u>.

1. This digital camera is broken. It's also out-of-date.

   <u>This digital camera is broken and out-of-date.</u> _____

2. I hear Econotech scanners are good. They're affordable, too.

   _____

3. Microwaves are fast, and they are convenient.

   _____

4. These coffee makers are expensive, but they are guaranteed.

   _____

5. I'm looking for an up-to-date smart phone. And I'd like it to be small.

   _____

C Look at the ad. Then write short answers to the questions.

My Buddy 266T

Portable GPS

with touch screen
free traffic updates

$299.99

1. What is it? _____

2. What brand is it? _____

3. What model is it? _____

4. What does it do? _____

5. What adjectives describe it? _____

6. Where do you use it? _____

7. Is it a good product? Why or why not? _____

D Write a paragraph describing the product from Exercise C.

Staying in Shape

1 **Look at the pictures. Name each activity. Write the letter on the line.**

Ⓐ Ⓑ Ⓒ Ⓓ Ⓔ Ⓕ Ⓖ Ⓗ Ⓘ

_____ 1. swimming	_____ 4. dancing	_____ 7. running
_____ 2. walking	_____ 5. playing soccer	_____ 8. lifting weights
_____ 3. doing aerobics	_____ 6. cooking dinner	_____ 9. sleeping

2 **Choose the correct response. Write the letter on the line.**

1. Kate has ballet class on Mondays. She goes to ballet _____ .   **a.** almost never

2. The first thing I do in the morning is drink coffee. I drink coffee _____ .   **b.** every weekend

3. I play basketball, but not as much as I'd like to. I _____ play.   **c.** never

4. Anna's husband does all the cooking. Anna _____ cooks.   **d.** every day

5. Jim and Dean always play golf on Saturday or Sunday. They play golf _____ .   **e.** once a week

3 **How often do you do these activities? Complete the chart.**

Activity	How often?
ride a bike	
eat in a restaurant	
shop for clothes	
shop for food	
watch TV	
clean your house	
exercise	

4 **Answer the questions. Use your own words.**

1. "What are you up to?"

   (YOU) _____

2. "Are you in shape or out of shape?"

   (YOU) _____

3. "What are you crazy about?"

   (YOU) _____

5 Complete the sentences. Use <u>have to</u> or <u>has to</u>.

1. I _____ go to class this morning. Do you have my textbook?

2. She can sleep late tomorrow. She doesn't _____ work until 10:30.

3. My brother isn't healthy. He _____ exercise more.

4. They don't _____ pick us up at the train station. We can take a taxi.

5. Pete _____ buy a new digital camera. His old one isn't working.

6. Do you _____ work next Saturday?

7. We _____ finish our report before the next sales meeting.

6 Write sentences. Use words from each box.

I My parents My teacher My friend My boss My brother	**+**	has to don't have to can can't have to doesn't have to	**+**	work late on Friday. play tennis this weekend. go to school. study English. go shopping this weekend. cook dinner tonight. sleep late tomorrow morning.

1. <u>My brother doesn't have to study English.</u> _____

2. _____

3. _____

4. _____

5. _____

7 Look at the responses. Write questions with <u>can</u> or <u>have to</u>.

1. **A:** (Gail / speak Polish) <u>Can Gail speak Polish</u>_____?
   B: No. She speaks English and French.

2. **A:** (you / play basketball tonight) _____?
   B: Sure. I'm not busy.

3. **A:** (you / meet your brother at the airport) _____?
   B: No, I don't. He's taking a bus.

4. **A:** (I / call you tomorrow) _____?
   B: OK. That would be great.

5. **A:** (Frank / buy a new printer) _____?
   B: No. He fixed his old one.

6. **A:** (they / take the exam on Friday) _____?
   B: Yes, they do. They're studying tonight.

8 Look at Paula's daily planner. Answer the questions about her schedule.

1. Can Paula go running Saturday morning at 9:00?
   No, she can't. She has to study English.

2. What does Paula have to do on Sunday afternoon?
   _____

3. Does Paula have to work on Friday?
   _____

4. Why can't Paula do aerobics Sunday night at 7:30?
   _____

5. Can Paula sleep late on Sunday morning?
   _____

Daily Planner

	FRIDAY	SATURDAY	SUNDAY
9:00	Arrive at the office	English class	
11:00			
1:00	Sales meeting	Lunch with Dad	Clean the house
3:00			
5:00	Leave the office	Shop for a new cell phone	Cook dinner
7:00	Do aerobics		See a movie with Sara

9 Choose the correct response. Circle the letter.

1. "Why don't we go bike riding this weekend?"
   a. Too bad. b. Sounds good. c. Don't bother.

2. "I'd love to go dancing with you sometime."
   a. When's good for you? b. Want to come along? c. What are you up to?

3. "When's good for you?"
   a. Sorry, I can't. b. How about Thursday? c. Once a week.

4. "Saturday at noon is perfect."
   a. I'm sorry to hear that. b. Well, how about Sunday? c. Great. See you then.

LESSON 2

10 Complete the sentences with places from the box.

gym	athletic field	pool	court	track	course

1. The school _____ is used for a lot of different sports. Students play football and soccer in the fall and baseball in the spring.

2. You can take an aerobics class or use exercise machines at a _____ .

3. The hotel has a tennis _____ and an 18-hole golf _____ .

4. On Fridays, there are water aerobics classes in the swimming _____ .

5. You can go running or walking on a _____ .

11 Look at Dave's activity schedule for September. Then complete the sentences. Circle the letter.

Dave's Activity Schedule   *September*

Sunday	Monday	Tuesday	Wednesday	Thursday	Friday	Saturday
	1 lift weights at the gym 5:30 PM	**2**	**3** play basketball 7:00 PM	**4** lift weights at the gym 5:30 PM	**5** study English 8:45 PM	**6** lift weights at the gym 5:30 PM
7 clean the house 10:00 AM	**8** lift weights at the gym 5:30 PM	**9** lift weights at the gym 5:30 PM	**10** play basketball 7:00 PM	**11** lift weights at the gym 5:30 PM	**12** study English 8:45 PM	**13** go running at the track 12:00 PM
14 clean the house 10:00 AM	**15** go running at the track 7:00 PM	**16** lift weights at the gym 5:30 PM	**17** play basketball 7:00 PM	**18** lift weights at the gym 5:30 PM	**19**	**20** lift weights at the gym 10:00 AM play golf 3:00 PM
21 clean the house 10:00 AM lift weights at the gym 1:00 PM	**22** lift weights at the gym 5:30 PM	**23** lift weights at the gym 5:30 PM	**24** play basketball 7:00 PM	**25** lift weights at the gym 5:30 PM	**26** study English 8:45 PM	**27** go bike riding 5:00 PM
28 clean the house 10:00 AM	**29** lift weights at the gym 5:30 PM	**30**				

1. Dave _____ goes bike riding.
  a. hardly ever   **b.** never   **c.** always

2. Dave _____ cleans the house on Sundays.
  a. always   **b.** sometimes   **c.** never

3. Dave lifts weights _____.
  a. once a week   **b.** at least three times a week   **c.** every day

4. Dave plays basketball _____.
  a. on Tuesdays   **b.** on Wednesdays   **c.** on weekends

5. Dave usually lifts weights _____.
  a. in the evening   **b.** in the morning   **c.** in the afternoon

6. Dave _____ goes running.
  a. once a month   **b.** every weekend   **c.** almost never

12 Write sentences about your own activities.

Examples: _I eat in a restaurant every weekend._
I almost never ride a bike.

1. _____
2. _____
3. _____
4. _____
5. _____

13 Look at the responses. Complete the questions. Use the simple present tense.

1. A: How often _does Jim play tennis_____?
   B: Jim almost never plays tennis.

2. A: How often _____?
   B: I go walking every day.

3. A: When _____?
   B: I usually cook dinner at 7:00.

4. A: When _____?
   B: They go dancing on Friday nights.

5. A: Where _____?
   B: We do aerobics at the gym.

6. A: Where _____?
   B: Kyle plays soccer at the athletic field.

14 Write sentences. Use the simple present tense or the present continuous.

1. Charlie / usually / play golf / on weekends
   _Charlie usually plays golf on weekends._____

2. Adam / talk on the phone / right now

   _____

3. My stepbrother / hardly ever / clean the house

   _____

4. We / go dancing / tonight

   _____

5. I / sleep late / tomorrow morning

   _____

6. Cindy / go swimming / twice a week

   _____

7. Deanna / almost always / watch TV / on weeknights

   _____

8. They / work late / next Tuesday

   _____

15 Choose the correct response. Write the letter on the line.

_____ 1. "How often do you do aerobics?"

_____ 2. "Where are you off to?"

_____ 3. "How often do you go swimming?"

_____ 4. "When do you go dancing?"

_____ 5. "How come you're not going running tonight?"

_____ 6. "Are you studying right now?"

a. Because I'm too busy.

b. No, I'm not. I'm watching TV.

c. I go to the gym once a week.

d. I hardly ever go to the pool.

e. On Friday nights.

f. I'm meeting my sister at the pool in 15 minutes.

LESSONS 3 and 4

16 Read the letters to a health magazine advice column.

Dear In-Shape,

I have two health questions for you. I'm an athlete. I play baseball for my university team, and I go running every day. I exercise all the time. I think I'm in terrific shape, but I'm worried that I exercise too much. That's my first question—how much exercise is too much?

My second question is about my diet. I try to eat healthy. I hardly ever eat pizza, fast food, or other snacks. I never drink soft drinks. But I have one really bad habit: I have a sweet tooth! I eat too much chocolate, candy, cake, and ice cream. How can I cut down on sweets?

—Ron Miller

Dear In-Shape,

I need some exercise advice! I don't feel very healthy. I get tired just walking from my house to my car! My doctor said that I have to exercise more. I'm sure that she's right. I should get out of the house more often. My husband goes running every day, but I never go running with him. I'm a couch potato. My big activity is watching movies—I watch a movie just about every night. Unfortunately, you don't burn many calories watching TV!

By the way, the problem is not my diet. I generally try to eat foods that are good for me, like fish, vegetables, and fruit. I avoid snacks, and I almost never eat sweets!

—Nina Hunter

Now read the letters on page 55 again. Complete the chart about Ron's and Nina's diet and exercise habits. Check the boxes.

	Ron Miller	Nina Hunter
is in shape	☐	☐
is out of shape	☐	☐
eats junk food	☐	☐
avoids sweets	☐	☐
is crazy about sweets	☐	☐

17 Read the sentences about Ron and Nina. Check <u>true</u>, <u>false</u>, or <u>no information</u>.

	true	false	no information
1. Ron doesn't have time to exercise.	☐	☐	☐
2. Ron generally avoids junk food.	☐	☐	☐
3. Ron usually drinks a lot of water.	☐	☐	☐
4. Nina never eats fish.	☐	☐	☐
5. Nina doesn't exercise regularly.	☐	☐	☐
6. Nina doesn't eat healthy foods.	☐	☐	☐

18 Are you in shape? Do you have a healthy diet? Explain your answers.

I don't have a healthy diet. I almost never eat vegetables . . .

19 Read the articles on page 70 of the Student's Book again. Answer the questions.

EXTRA READING
COMPREHENSION

1. Why can't Mark Zupan move his arms and legs normally? _____

2. What is Zupan's nickname? _____

3. What sport does he play? _____

4. What does he do to stay in shape? _____

5. What does he do in his free time? _____

6. What is Bethany Hamilton's sport? _____

7. How did Hamilton lose her arm? _____

8. What does she do when she's not surfing? _____

9. What is her advice? _____

A Rewrite each sentence. Use <u>can</u> or <u>can't</u>.

1. Eric is going surfing this weekend.

Eric can go surfing this weekend. _____

2. Tana and Glenn aren't playing golf on Sunday.

_____

3. Are we sleeping late tomorrow?

_____

4. My stepsister isn't going to the movies with us.

_____

B Rewrite each sentence. Use <u>have to</u> or <u>don't have to</u>.

1. We're cleaning the house on Saturday.

We have to clean the house on Saturday. _____

2. Are the salespeople working late tonight?

_____

3. Kelly and Caroline are studying for the test tomorrow.

_____

4. We're not buying a new printer.

_____

C Look at the responses. Write information questions with <u>can</u>.

1. A: *Where can I go running* _____?
   B: Well, you can run in the park.

2. A: _____?
   B: I think she can come after class, but I'm not sure.

3. A: _____?
   B: Three. I speak Spanish, English, and Japanese.

4. A: _____?
   B: I can meet you at 9:30.

5. A: _____?
   B: Not very often. Golf is so expensive around here.

D Look at the responses. Write information questions with <u>have to</u>.

1. **A:** <u>How often do you have to</u> _____ see your doctor?
   B: Not very often. Just once a year.

2. **A:** _____ meet the client tomorrow?
   B: I have to meet him at the airport.

3. **A:** _____ pick up the car?
   B: You have to pick it up before 5:00. They close early today.

4. **A:** _____ work late tonight?
   B: Because she has a big meeting tomorrow.

5. **A:** _____ get at the supermarket?
   B: We need to get some chicken and broccoli for dinner tonight.

E Complete the sentences. Circle the letter.

1. I _____ about lunch. What do you want?
   a. think   **b.** am thinking   **c.** thinks

2. He _____ her very much now.
   a. love   **b.** is loving   **c.** loves

3. Michelle can't come to the phone. She _____.
   a. sleep   **b.** sleeping   **c.** is sleeping

4. They _____ the chef at that restaurant.
   a. are knowing   **b.** know   **c.** am knowing

5. We _____ some soup for dinner. Would you like some?
   a. am having   **b.** has   **c.** are having

F Unscramble the words to write sentences in the simple present tense.

1. she / a lot / swimming / not / go
   <u>She doesn't go swimming a lot.</u>

2. walk / Joel / to school / sometimes
   _____

3. always / my sisters / on the weekend / me / call
   _____

4. every day / meet / not / their / class
   _____

5. cook dinner / not / usually / on Friday nights / I
   _____

6. they / three times a week / play tennis / generally
   _____

A **Correct the capitalization and punctuation in the sentences.**

1. I'm crazy about basketball, soccer, and golf.

2. my stepbrother burns more than 3000 calories a day

3. sometimes i have a candy bar for lunch

4. how often do you exercise

5. max hates to play sports but he loves to watch sports on tv

6. what do you generally eat for breakfast

7. they have to clean the house go shopping and study on weekends

8. is there a park a track or an athletic field near your home

9. rose avoids red meat junk food soda and sweets

10. how many hours do you usually sleep

B **Choose two questions from Exercise A. Rewrite the questions with correct capitalization and punctuation and write your own answers. Explain your answers.**

Q:

A:

Q:

A:

1 Match the activities for Dublin, Ireland, with the types of interests. Write the letter on the line.

_____ **1.** play golf on an island in Dublin Bay

_____ **2.** enjoy fresh, local seafood

_____ **3.** see the 1,200-year-old Book of Kells at Trinity College

_____ **4.** visit the Dublin Zoo in Phoenix Park

_____ **5.** watch a performance of traditional Irish music and dance

a. history

b. entertainment

c. physical activities

d. good food

e. family activities

2 What do you like to do on vacation? Number the boxes in order, making number 1 your favorite.

_____ take pictures   _____ swim   _____ go snorkeling

_____ go shopping   _____ lie in the sun   _____ walk around and explore

_____ eat in restaurants   _____ watch movies or shows   _____ go to clubs

_____ visit museums   _____ walk on the beach   _____ play golf

3 In your country, where would you go on vacation for . . .

good food and entertainment?	history and culture?
family activities?	physical activities?

Trinity College in Dublin, Ireland

60

4 Complete the conversations. Write the best response on the lines. Use sentences from the box.

I'm fine, thanks.	That's too bad.	It was pretty long and boring.
Well, that's good.	Not too bad, actually.	

Can I give you a hand?

1. _____ _____

2. _____ _____

So how was the trip?

I'll bet the food was terrible.

3. _____ _____

Of course, the train wasn't on time.

4. _____ _____

But it was very scenic.

5. _____ _____

5 Write statements. Use the words in parentheses and <u>was</u>, <u>were</u>, <u>wasn't</u>, or <u>weren't</u>.

1. (The cruise / terrific) *The cruise was terrific.*_____

2. (The shops / quite nice) _____

3. (Our room / really small) _____

4. (There / not / many family activities) _____

5. (There / a lot of friendly people) _____

6. (The flight / not / very long) _____

6 Write <u>yes</u> / <u>no</u> questions and short answers. Use the past tense of <u>be</u>.

1. **A:** (your / bus trip / long) *Was your bus trip long*_____ ?
   B: No, *it wasn't* . It was less than an hour.

2. **A:** (the movie theater / open) _____ ?
   B: Yes, _____ . They had a late show.

3. **A:** (the weather / good) _____ ?
   B: No, _____ . It rained every day.

4. **A:** (there / a movie / on your flight) _____ ?
   B: No, _____ . It was so boring!

5. **A:** (there / many people / on the train) _____ ?
   B: Yes, _____ . We had to stand.

7 Complete the conversation with information questions.
Use the past tense of <u>be</u>.

A: Hey, Marty. _____ ?
          1. Where / you / last weekend
B: My wife and I took a little vacation.

A: Really? _____ ?
                  2. How / it
B: Too short! But we stayed at a great resort.

A: Oh yeah? _____ ?
                 3. Where / the resort
B: Over in Wroxton. We drove up Friday night.

A: Wroxton? That's rather far. _____ ?
                                  4. How long / the drive
B: About three and a half hours. There wasn't any traffic.

A: Nice! _____ ?
            5. And / how / the weather
B: Actually, the weather was quite good. Only rained once!

A: Sounds wonderful. _____ ?
                         6. How long / you / there
B: Just three days. We didn't want to come home!

8 Answer the questions. Use your own words.

1. "When was your last trip?" (YOU) _____

2. "How was the trip?" (YOU) _____

3. "How was the weather?" (YOU) _____

9 Complete the chart with the present or simple past tense.

	Present tense	Simple past tense
1.	call	
2.		arrived
3.		studied
4.	get	
5.	stop	

	Present tense	Simple past tense
6.		went
7.	buy	
8.	do	
9.	leave	
10.		ate

10 Complete the sentences with the simple past tense.

1. I _____ some nice souvenirs, but I _____
  buy   not spend
a lot of money.

2. We _____ to Montreal, but we _____
  fly   take
the train back.

3. We _____ a great time at the baseball game!
  have
The kids _____ hot dogs and _____ soda,
  eat   drink
and they _____ the game, too—a little!
  watch

4. I _____ on Friday night. I _____ back at
  leave   get
noon on Sunday.

11 Read the responses. Write questions in the simple past tense, using the
words in parentheses. Use question words when necessary.

1. A: (you / eat) _Where did you eat_ _____?
   B: We ate at a Japanese restaurant.

2. A: (you / go with) _____?
   B: I went with Janine.

3. A: (you / like / the art exhibit) _____?
   B: No, I didn't. It was kind of boring.

4. A: (you / leave) _____?
   B: We left on Tuesday morning.

5. A: (she / buy) _____?
   B: She bought some T-shirts.

6. A: (he / play tennis) _____?
   B: He played at the courts at his hotel.

7. A: (you / stay) _____?
   B: We stayed a little over a month.

12 Choose the correct responses to complete the conversation. Write the letter on the line.

A: Hi, Emily. I didn't see you at the gym last week.

B: _____
   1.

A: Really? Where did you go?

B: _____
   2.

A: No kidding! How was it?

B: _____
   3.

A: That sounds incredible. Did you and your husband get to go out?

B: _____
   4.

a. We visited my sister in California and took the kids to Disneyland.

b. Yes, we did. My sister baby-sat, and we ate at some really nice restaurants.

c. I didn't go. We were on vacation.

d. Fantastic. The kids had so much fun.

13 Answer the questions. Use your own words.

1. "Where did you go on your last vacation?"

   YOU _____

2. "Did you have a good time?"

   YOU _____

3. "What did you do?"

   YOU _____

LESSONS 3 and 4

14 Read the vacation reviews on page 80 of the Student's Book again. Circle T for <u>true</u> or F for <u>false</u> about each statement. Find words in the text to support your answers.

EXTRA READING
COMPREHENSION

(T) F **1.** The spa vacation in Bali was relaxing.
   . . . on healthy living and meditation. It was so quiet there! _____

T F **2.** The Victoria Falls vacation was boring.

   _____

T F **3.** Jason K. and his wife are not going back to Bali again.

   _____

T F **4.** Paula B. didn't think Victoria Falls was awesome.

   _____

T F **5.** There wasn't time for shopping on Arturo Manuel R.'s trip.

   _____

T F **6.** Jason K. and his wife enjoyed healthy food in Bali.

   _____

15 Look at the vacation picture.

Now read the statements. Who is speaking? Match each statement to a person in the picture. Write the letter on the line.

We ate at the hotel restaurant. The food was awful.

1. _____

I got a massage on the beach. It was so relaxing!

4. _____

Someone stole my bag! I lost all of my money and my passport.

2. _____

The entertainment was terrible. They only had one musician— and he needed guitar lessons!

5. _____

I went parasailing. A boat pulled me up high in the air. It was really exciting!

3. _____

The local beverages were terrific. I had a drink made of coconut milk every day at the beach.

6. _____

16 Complete the vacation postcard. Use adjectives from the box.

| scary | relaxing | perfect | terrible | scenic | unusual |

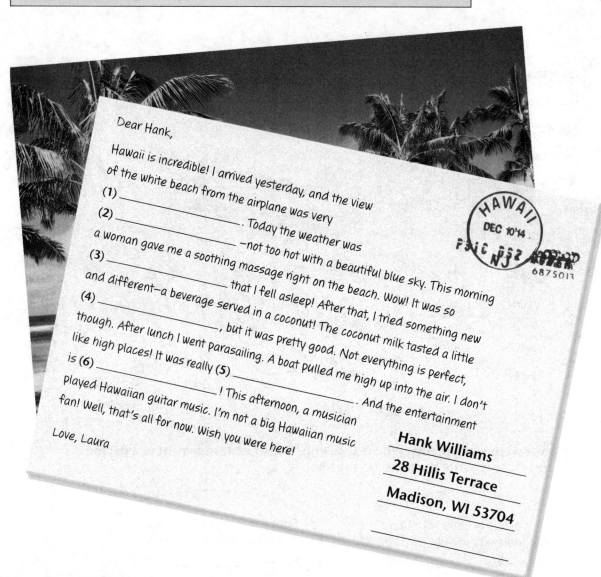

Dear Hank,

Hawaii is incredible! I arrived yesterday, and the view
of the white beach from the airplane was very
(1) _____. Today the weather was
(2) _____ —not too hot with a beautiful blue sky. This morning
a woman gave me a soothing massage right on the beach. Wow! It was so
(3) _____ that I fell asleep! After that, I tried something new
and different—a beverage served in a coconut! The coconut milk tasted a little
(4) _____, but it was pretty good. Not everything is perfect,
though. After lunch I went parasailing. A boat pulled me high up into the air. I don't
like high places! It was really (5) _____. And the entertainment
is (6) _____! This afternoon, a musician
played Hawaiian guitar music. I'm not a big Hawaiian music
fan! Well, that's all for now. Wish you were here!

Love, Laura

Hank Williams

28 Hillis Terrace

Madison, WI 53704

_____

GRAMMAR BOOSTER

A Choose the correct response. Write the letter on the line.

_____ 1. "How was your vacation?"

_____ 2. "Where did you go?"

_____ 3. "How long were you there?"

_____ 4. "Was the weather good?"

_____ 5. "How were the rooms?"

_____ 6. "Were there a lot of things to do?"

_____ 7. "Was the food OK?"

a. No, it wasn't. It rained all week.

b. Terrific. It was so much fun.

c. Jamaica.

d. Yes, there were. We were busy all the time.

e. Yes, it was good. But a little spicy.

f. Just a week.

g. Clean and comfortable.

B Correct the errors in the e-mail message.

Dear Mari,

My vacation ~~were~~ *was* lots of fun! My family and I went to Hawaii. The only problem were the hotel. It was very nice. The beds were terrible. Everything else were perfect. There was many activities. My favorite activity wasn't parasailing. It were terrific.

Laura

C Write questions with the past tense of <u>be</u>. Then answer the questions with complete sentences. Use your own words.

1. when / your last vacation _____?

   YOU _____

2. it / long _____?

   YOU _____

3. the hotel / nice _____?

   YOU _____

4. how / the weather _____?

   YOU _____

5. how many / people / with you _____?

   YOU _____

D Complete the paragraph. Use the simple past tense of words from the box. Some words can be used more than once.

drink	stop	travel	take	shop	watch	be	walk

In January, I _____ to Morocco with my friend Nan. We explored
          1.
the narrow streets of the medieval medina in Marrakech. The medina is closed to

traffic. So, there _____ no cars, but there _____ a lot of donkeys.
          2.   3.
We _____ for hours and _____ often to look at the beautiful
       4.   5.
carpets for sale. We _____ for inexpensive leather goods, _____
              6.   7.
mint tea, and _____ street performers. We wandered all afternoon. We
       8.
got lost, and then we _____ a taxi back to our hotel.
              9.

E Rewrite the sentences. Use the simple past tense and a past time expression.

1. We go to the beach every year. <u>We went to the beach last year.</u>
2. The weather isn't very nice today. _____
3. We don't stay in a hotel. _____
4. I often cook clams at the beach. _____
5. Everyone has a good time. _____
6. What do you do in the summer? _____

F Read the statements. Write questions to ask for more information, using the words in parentheses.

1. **A:** She bought a new printer. **B:** <u>Why did she buy a new printer</u> ? (why)
2. **A:** She went on vacation. **B:** _____ ? (where)
3. **A:** They went to the gym. **B:** _____ ? (when)
4. **A:** I visited some friends. **B:** _____ ? (who)
5. **A:** He spent a lot of money. **B:** _____ ? (how much)

WRITING BOOSTER

A Read the sentences about Amy's weekend trip to Chicago with her girlfriends.

1. They all flew to Chicago and met at the airport.
2. They checked into their hotel downtown and got dressed to go out.
3. They saw the musical *Jersey Boys*.
4. On Saturday, they went to the spa and got massages.
5. They went shopping on Michigan Avenue.
6. They had a delicious steak dinner at a nice restaurant.
7. They listened to jazz music at an uptown club.
8. They went out dancing.
9. They said good-bye and returned home on Sunday.

B On a separate sheet of paper, write a paragraph about Amy's trip. Use time clauses and time-order transition words.

Let me tell you about Amy's trip to Chicago with her girlfriends. First, . . .

The Top 10 Most Visited Tourist Attractions in the World

1. Times Square—New York City (U.S.)
2. National Mall & Memorial Parks—Washington, D.C. (U.S.)
3. Disney World's Magic Kingdom—Orlando, Florida (U.S.)
4. Trafalgar Square—London (U.K.)
5. Disneyland Park—Anaheim, California (U.S.)
6. Niagara Falls—Canada and U.S.
7. Fisherman's Wharf—San Francisco, California (U.S.)
8. Tokyo Disneyland—Tokyo (Japan)
9. Notre Dame Cathedral—Paris (France)
10. Disneyland—Paris (France)

Shopping for Clothes

1 Label each clothing item with the correct department. Use words from the box.
Write the letter on the line.

a. Sleepwear	**c. Athletic Wear**	**e. Hosiery**
b. Underwear & Lingerie	**d. Outerwear**	**f. Bags & Accessories**

_____ 1. coats

_____ 2. sunglasses

_____ 3. slippers

_____ 4. golf shirts

_____ 5. slips

_____ 6. pantyhose

2 What's important to these customers when they shop for footwear?
Write <u>price</u>, <u>selection</u>, or <u>service</u> on the line.

I always shop at Dalton's Department Store because the clerks are really helpful. They always help me find the right size and even offer to gift wrap!

I'm a student so I don't have a lot of money. I shop at Shoe Outlet because they always have a big sale. The shoes I'm wearing now were 50% off!

Jake's Footwear is the best! They have more than 200 different kinds of footwear—boots, sandals, running shoes . . . I like to have a lot of choices when I shop.

1. _____

2. _____

3. _____

3 Label the clothing items in the picture. Use words from the box.

| pumps |
| running shoes |
| a sweatshirt |
| a blazer |
| a shirt |
| a windbreaker |
| pantyhose |
| a skirt |
| socks |
| sweatpants |

1. _____

2. _____

3. _____

4. _____

5. _____

6. _____

7. _____

8. _____

9. _____

10. _____

4 What's your style? Complete the chart with the clothing and shoes you usually wear.

At home	At work	At school	To go out

5 Complete the conversations. Use object pronouns from the box. Pronouns can be used more than once.

me	you	him	her	it	us	them

1. **A:** Are your sisters going to the party?

   B: I hope so. I invited _____ .

2. **A:** This sweatshirt is really old.

   B: That's OK. I wear _____ to exercise.

3. **A:** Did you meet Ms. Jacobs?

   B: Yes, I met _____ this morning.

4. **A:** When can I call you?

   B: Let's see. Call _____ tomorrow. I'll be home all day.

5. **A:** I didn't see you and Emma at the concert.

   B: You didn't see _____ ? We were right near the stage.

6. **A:** I'll take the sandals.

   B: Great. Would you like me to gift wrap _____ for _____ ?

7. **A:** These pants are too small.

   B: Give _____ to your brother.

   A: I can't give _____ to _____ . He wears a size 36!

6 Complete the conversations. Use sentences from the box.

| Credit, please. | That's too bad. | Certainly. | The V-neck or the crew neck? |

Could you gift wrap these shirts?

1. _____ _____

Did you know that...
- the first known pictures of footwear are boots in a 15,000-year-old painting in a cave in Spain?
- in the year 200, Marcus Aurelius, Emperor of Rome, said that only he could wear red sandals?
- before the 1860s, pairs of boots didn't have a right and a left? Both boots were the same.

How would you like to pay?

2. _____ _____

I'm sorry. We don't have these pumps in black.

3. _____ _____

I'll take the sweater.

4. _____ _____

LESSON **2**

7 Complete the chart with words from the box. Write the comparative form of each adjective in the correct column.

loose	spicy	hot	sweet	comfortable
tall	bad	important	thin	young
friendly	healthy	nice	fat	convenient

1. (+) -r	2. (+) -er	3. (–) -y (+) -ier	4. double the final consonant (+) -er	5. more	6. irregular forms
larger	smaller	heavier	bigger	more expensive	better
					X
X					X

8 Compare the items in the pictures. Write sentences with comparative adjectives. Use words from the box or your own words.

spicy	salty	expensive	portable	young
old	cheap	fast	healthy	large
big	small	comfortable	good	convenient

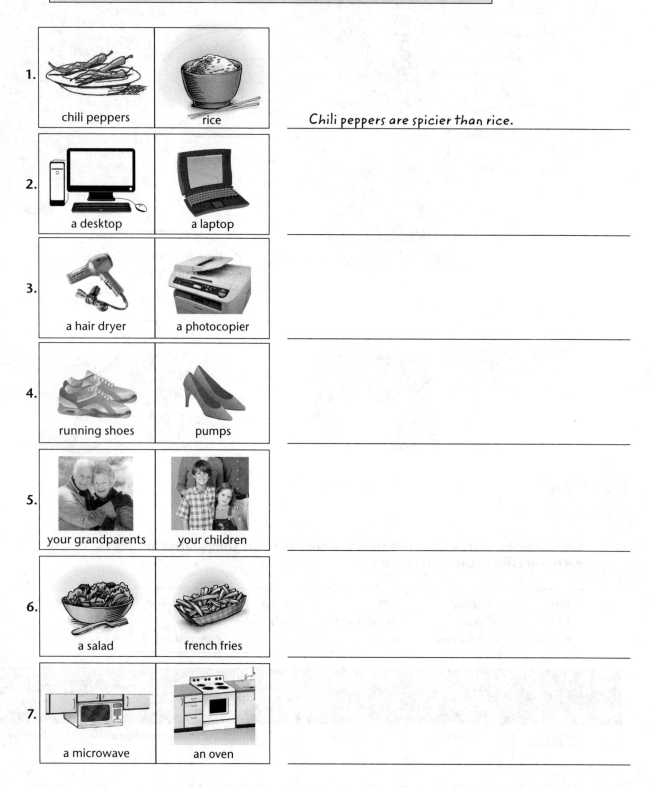

1. chili peppers / rice

   Chili peppers are spicier than rice.

2. a desktop / a laptop

3. a hair dryer / a photocopier

4. running shoes / pumps

5. your grandparents / your children

6. a salad / french fries

7. a microwave / an oven

9 Choose the correct response. Circle the letter.

1. "Do you have this in a medium?"
   a. Thanks.
   b. Here you go.
   c. Yes, please.

2. "How much are these pajamas?"
   a. The Dreams brand ones?
   b. That's not too bad.
   c. These are a large.

3. "Can I try it on?"
   a. Yes, we do.
   b. No, thanks.
   c. Of course!

4. "Thank you for wrapping them for me."
   a. They're $75.
   b. My pleasure.
   c. Yes, please.

10 Look at the store ad. Then complete the sentences. Use the information in the ad or your own words.

1. The Comfort brand boots are _____ than the Downtown boots.

2. The Big City Footwear store has the Arctic brand boots in brown and _____ .

3. The Downtown brand boots are _____ than the Arctic brand boots.

4. The Arctic brand boots are _____ than the Comfort brand boots.

5. The Big City Footwear store has the Downtown brand boots in sizes _____ .

11 Complete the sentences. Use your own ideas and the cues in parentheses.

1. _____ is more expensive than _____ . (two clothing stores)

2. _____ is better than _____ . (two restaurants)

3. _____ is more popular than _____ . (two music genres)

4. _____ is warmer than _____ . (two travel destinations)

5. _____ is more exciting than _____ . (two physical activities)

12 **Look at the store floor plan. Start at the Information desk. Follow the directions. Where are you? Write the name of the department on the line.**

1. That's on this floor. Walk to the back of the store. It's on the left side, just past Hosiery.

   Where are you?

   _____

2. Take the elevator to the second floor. Turn left when you get off. Then turn right at Men's Outerwear. It's between Men's Outerwear and Men's Underwear.

   Where are you?

   _____

3. Go down the escalator to the basement and walk to the front of the store. You'll see it on the right.

   Where are you?

   _____

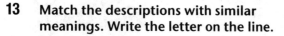

13 **Match the descriptions with similar meanings. Write the letter on the line.**

_____ 1. informal   **a.** modest

_____ 2. liberal   **b.** casual

_____ 3. conservative   **c.** showing too much skin

_____ 4. revealing   **d.** "anything goes"

EXTRA READING COMPREHENSION

14 **Read the travel blog on page 94 of the Student's Book again. What clothing is appropriate for women traveling in Turkey? What about in the United States? Choose one of these countries and complete the chart of do's and don'ts.**

Country: _____

Do's	Don'ts

15 Choose one of the travel destinations below. What clothing will you pack for the trip? Make a list. Include any shoes, outerwear, casual, formal, conservative, or wild clothes you will need.

Go skiing in the Swiss Alps.	Hear gospel music at a Harlem church in New York City, USA.	Go dancing at a nightclub in Paris, France.	Go swimming on Boracay Island, Philippines.

GRAMMAR BOOSTER

A Write questions to ask for more information. Use object pronouns and the words in parentheses.

1. **A:** I take my grandmother to the same restaurant every week.
   B: _Where do you take her_ ? (where)

2. **A:** She washes her car a lot.
   B: _____? (when)

3. **A:** He eats sandwiches for lunch.
   B: _____? (how often)

4. **A:** Monica meets her boyfriend for coffee every day.
   B: _____? (what time)

B Write sentences in two ways, using the words indicated. Add prepositions if necessary.

1. the address / give / her
   Give her the address.
   Give the address to her.

2. Tina / gifts / him / buys
   _____
   _____

3. the teacher / homework / us / gave
   _____
   _____

4. the waiters / them / their lunch / served
   _____
   _____

5. Ann / a shirt / her son / bought
   _____
   _____

6. the clerk / me / a smaller size / found
   _____
   _____

C Complete the sentences with words from the box. Use the comparative form.

relaxing	healthy	comfortable	nice	warm	fast	big

1. A turtleneck is _____ than a V-neck.

2. Flats are _____ than pumps.

3. Athletic fields are usually _____ than tennis courts.

4. Salads are _____ than fries.

5. The expensive suit isn't _____ than the inexpensive one. It's just more expensive.

6. I don't like to fly, but it's _____ than taking the train.

7. A spa vacation is _____ than a business trip.

D Answer the questions in complete sentences. Use your own words.

1. "Which is easier—speaking or writing in English?"

   YOU _____

2. "Where are you happier—at home or on vacation?"

   YOU _____

3. "Which is more interesting—shopping for clothes or shopping for electronics?"

   YOU _____

WRITING BOOSTER

A Check the sentence with the clearer meaning.

1. ☐ We're going to a restaurant since we don't have any food at home.
   ☐ We don't have any food at home since we're going to a restaurant.

2. ☐ We're going to the beach because I packed my swimsuit.
   ☐ I packed my swimsuit because we're going to the beach.

3. ☐ Because we're shopping for a new one, our computer is obsolete.
   ☐ Because our computer is obsolete, we're shopping for a new one.

4. ☐ Since he didn't have cash, he used his credit card.
   ☐ Since he used his credit card, he didn't have cash.

B Answer each of the following questions with a complete sentence containing a clause with <u>because</u> or <u>since</u>. Use your own words.

   Example: Do you like shopping for clothes online?

   <u>I don't like shopping for clothes online because I can't try them on.</u>

1. "Do you like going to concerts?"

   YOU _____

2. "Which is better—a large family or a small family?"

   YOU _____

3. "Do you like eating at home or eating in a restaurant?"

   YOU _____

4. "When you go on vacation, do you like going to big cities or small towns?"

   YOU _____

9 Taking Transportation

1 Look at the departure schedule and the clock. Read the statements. Check true or false.

		true	false
1.	The next flight to Porto Alegre is at 5:50 P.M.	☐	☐
2.	Flight 902 to São Luis is leaving from Gate G4.	☐	☐
3.	The flight to Caracas is delayed.	☐	☐
4.	Flight number 267 is going to Belo Horizonte.	☐	☐
5.	Passengers traveling to Rio de Janeiro on Flight 89 should hurry.	☐	☐
6.	Flight 60 to São Paulo is late.	☐	☐

RAPID AIR BRASILIA DEPARTURES

Destination	FLT/No.	Departs	Gate	Status
São Paulo	56	15:50	G4	departed
Belo Horizonte	267	16:10	G3	boarding
Rio de Janeiro	89	16:10	G9	boarding
São Paulo	58	16:50	G4	now 17:25
São Luis	902	17:00	G3	on time
São Paulo	60	17:50	G4	delayed
Porto Alegre	763	17:50	G3	on time
Caracas	04	18:05	G1	canceled
Rio de Janeiro	91	18:10	G9	on time
São Paulo	62	18:50	G4	on time

15:50

2 Choose the correct response. Write the letter on the line.

_____ 1. "Oh, no! The bus is leaving in four minutes."

_____ 2. "Good news. Our flight is on time."

_____ 3. "I'm looking for Gate C4."

_____ 4. "Is this your final destination?"

_____ 5. "I'm catching a flight to Barcelona, too."

_____ 6. "We're catching the 8:27 train, right?"

a. Thank goodness.

b. No, I'm connecting to Quito.

c. What a coincidence!

d. Yes. Let's look for track 6.

e. It's down this hall, on the right.

f. We should hurry!

LESSON 1

3 Answer the questions in complete sentences.

1. Which is faster—the local or the express?

_____

2. Which is more scenic—an aisle seat or a window seat?

_____

3. Which is more convenient—a direct flight or a non-stop flight?

_____

4. Which is less expensive—a one-way ticket or a round-trip ticket?

_____

4 **Complete each sentence or question. Use <u>could</u> or <u>should</u> and the base form of the verb.**

1. Want my advice? _____ the express. _____ the local, but it takes
   You / take   You / take
   thirty minutes longer.

2. _____! _____ the 7:30!
   You / hurry   You / make

3. _____ round-trip tickets. They are cheaper than two one-way tickets, and she won't
   She / buy
   have to wait in another ticket line.

4. _____ an aisle seat in the rear of the plane or a window seat in the front. What do
   We / take
   you think? Which seats _____ ?
   we / take

5. The flight is delayed. _____ late for the meeting. _____ the office?
   We / be   we / call

6. No, _____ a direct flight. They have to change planes in Anchorage.
   they / not / get

5 **Put the conversation in order. Write the number on the line.**

_____ Let's see. The local leaves from track 23, lower level.

_1_ Can I help you?

_____ Oh, no! What should we do?

_____ That's not too bad. What's the track number?

_____ Yes. Can we still make the 10:05 express to Antwerp?

_____ I'm sorry. You missed it.

_____ Thanks very much.

_____ Well, you could take a local train. There's one at 11:05.

6 **Look at the schedules. Which train should the people take? Write your advice on the line.**

Metropolitan Railroad			
	Local	**Express**	**Local**
White Plains	7:25	8:22	9:05
Scarsdale	7:42	-	9:22
Bronxville	8:05	-	9:40
Harlem 125th St.	8:24	-	9:59
Grand Central—New York City	8:30	8:59	10:06

I live in White Plains. I need a train that will arrive in New York City around 9:00 A.M. Could I take the 8:22 express?

1. _Yes, you could take the 8:22._

I live in White Plains. I'm meeting my boss at Grand Central Station at 8:45 A.M., and I can't be late. Which train should I take?

2. _____
   _____

I live in Scarsdale. I need to shop for a new laptop in New York City. Most computer stores open at 10:00 A.M. What time should I be at the Scarsdale train station?

3. _____
   _____

I'm in White Plains. I want to go to Bronxville. Could I take an express train? I want to get there quickly.

4. _____
   _____

7 What are your plans for today? Check the things you're going to do. Add your own activities.

☐ call a friend   ☐ check my e-mail   ☐ go shopping   ☐ study

☐ exercise   ☐ clean my house   ☐ take the bus   ☐ cook

☐ other _____

8 Now write sentences about your plans for today. Use the future tense with <u>be going to</u>.

I'm going to call a friend tonight after work.

9 What are they going to do? Write the letter on the line.

_____ **1.** She's going to make a reservation.   _____ **3.** She's going to take a limo.

_____ **2.** He's going to arrive at 8:45.   _____ **4.** He's not going to take a taxi.

10 Read the response. Complete each question with <u>be going to</u>.

1. **A:** Where _is Paul going to meet us_____?
   B: Paul's going to meet us at the airport café.

2. **A:** Who _____?
   B: I think Gretchen is going to buy the tickets.

3. **A:** When _____?
   B: I'm going to pack tonight.

4. **A:** What time _____?
   B: They're going to arrive at 5:50 P.M.

5. **A:** _____ our connecting flight?
   B: Yes, we'll make it.

> **Did you know?**
>
> The world's longest direct run train (without changing trains) is 10,214 km, from Moscow, Russia, to Pyongyang, North Korea. One train a week takes this route. The trip takes almost eight days!

11 Complete the conversation. Use words from the box.

limousine	going	should	late	check	arriving	reservation	rental

A: What time are we _____ in Copenhagen?
          1.
B: Pretty _____ . Around 10:30 P.M.
          2.
A: What about a hotel?
B: I'm going to make a _____ online.
          3.
A: Great. And are we _____ to need a taxi to the hotel?
          4.
B: There's a _____ from the airport, or we could
          5.
   get a _____ car.
          6.
A: They're expensive. We _____ save our money.
          7.
   Is there a train?
B: Let me _____ . . .
          8.

LESSONS 3 and 4

12 Complete the conversation. Use words from the box.

gate	make	check	land	delayed	depart
go through security		departure lounge		boarding passes	

1. **Passenger A:** Do we need to check in?
   Passenger B: No, we don't. I printed our _____ online, and we're not
                                                          1.
      checking any luggage.
   Passenger A: OK. Let's check a monitor for our _____ number, and then
                                                                      2.
      we should _____ .
                        3.

2. Passenger: Excuse me. Is Flight 68 going to _____ on time?
   _4._
   Agent: No, I'm sorry. The flight is _____ . Have a seat in the _____ .
   _5._   _6._
   We'll make an announcement when we're ready for boarding.

3. Passenger: Excuse me. What time are we going to _____ ?
   _7._
   Flight Attendant: Let me _____ . . . Our new arrival time is 8:23.
   _8._
   Passenger: 8:23? My connecting flight is at 8:40. Can I still _____ it?
   _9._

13 Read Bettine's blog entry.

Bettine's Blog
Transportation Troubles   posted May 12

Hi, everybody! Well, I'm back from my trip. Last week my husband and I flew to Boston, took a cruise ship to Quebec, took a bus to Montreal, and then flew home. Sounds like a dream vacation, right? Unfortunately my dream turned into a nightmare!

You won't believe what happened. First, our flight was delayed. The airplane had mechanical problems. We waited at the gate for two hours. After we finally took off, I closed my eyes for a nap, but sleeping was impossible. There was a terrible storm, and the flight was bumpy. It was pretty scary! I tried to watch a movie to stay calm, but the entertainment system wasn't working. The movie didn't have any sound.

The plane landed in Boston at 4:00 P.M.—three hours late. Our cruise ship was supposed to depart at 4:30! I ran to a taxi. My face was bright red from running as I gave the directions to the driver. "Please hurry," I added. Luckily, we arrived just in time. We didn't miss the ship!

I stood on the ship's deck and enjoyed the scenic views. However, the awful weather continued. I got seasick. Earlier, my face turned red from running.

On the deck, I turned green from the ship's motion. I was seasick the whole cruise!

What else could go wrong? A lot! Our bus to Montreal had an accident. No one was hurt, but we were delayed for an hour. Two days later, our flight home was overbooked. We got bumped from the plane and had to wait for the next flight.

As you can guess, I'm very happy to be home. However, I still have one big problem. The airline lost my luggage! Most of my clothing was in my bags, so now I have nothing to wear.

Are you looking for a relaxing vacation? Then I, Bettine, have some advice for you—you should stay home!

Now read the sentences. Check <u>true</u> or <u>false</u>.

		true	false
1.	Bettine's flight to Boston was delayed because of mechanical problems.	☐	☐
2.	Bettine was late, and she missed her cruise ship.	☐	☐
3.	The weather on Bettine's cruise was terrific.	☐	☐
4.	Bettine's bus to Montreal had an accident.	☐	☐
5.	Bettine got airsick on her flight home.	☐	☐
6.	Bettine thinks that traveling is relaxing.	☐	☐

14 Look at the pictures of Joe Kelly's trip. Then read the statements. Check <u>true</u> or <u>false</u>.

	true	false
1. His flight was on time.	☐	☐
2. He sat in an aisle seat.	☐	☐
3. His plane had mechanical problems.	☐	☐
4. He missed the hotel shuttle bus.	☐	☐
5. He drove a rental car to the hotel.	☐	☐

15 Write a short paragraph about Joe Kelly's trip.

16 Read the article "Got bumped from a flight?" on page 106 of the Student's Book again. Match words and phrases from their meanings.

_____ 1. overbook   a. have to get off the plane because there aren't enough seats

_____ 2. "no-shows"   b. someone who offers to get off an overbooked flight

_____ 3. get bumped   c. get off the plane

_____ 4. volunteer   d. sell too many tickets for a flight

_____ 5. perks   e. benefits like cash, free flights, hotels, and meals

_____ 6. deplane   f. people who have tickets but don't appear for a flight

17 Read the articles on page 106 of the Student's Book again. Answer the questions.

1. Why do airlines overbook flights?

   _____

2. What do airlines give bumped passengers?

   _____

3. Why did Mr. Carter turn onto the train tracks?

   _____

4. Were Mr. Carter and his son in the car when the train hit it?

   _____

5. What advice do the police officers give?

   _____

GRAMMAR BOOSTER

A Read the questions and statements. Correct the mistakes.

1. You should ~~to go~~ *go to* track 57.
2. Where could he to get a train to Paris?
3. Rebecca can't takes a flight to Tokyo.
4. When we should leave?
5. How late can he to board?
6. He shoulds choose an aisle seat.

B Read the questions. Complete the responses.

1. A: Should she take the local?
   B: No, *she shouldn't* _____. It's too slow.

2. A: Can he bring food on the flight?
   B: Yes, _____.

3. A: Could I take the number 3 train?
   B: Yes, _____. It will take you to the right station.

4. A: Can we get seats together?
   B: No, _____. I'm sorry. We only have a few seats left.

5. A: Should they get a rental car?
   B: Yes, _____. It's more convenient.

C Rewrite the sentences. Use a different way to express future actions. There may be more than one correct answer.

1. I'm studying all day tomorrow.

   _____

2. I'm going to run three miles on Saturday.

   _____

3. The train departs in twenty minutes.

   _____

4. The test is going to be next week.

   _____

5. The ship is going to arrive in Halifax tomorrow morning.

   _____

WRITING BOOSTER

A Think about two vacation destinations you know of and could recommend to others. Complete the chart.

	Destination 1	Destination 2
Where?		
How to get there?		
What time of year?		
What to see / do?		
What to bring?		
Where / What to eat?		
How long to stay?		

B On a separate sheet of paper, write two paragraphs about the vacation destinations you recommend. Give advice and suggest alternatives or possibilities. Use <u>should</u> and <u>could</u>. Start the first paragraph like this.

> I recommend _____ as your next vacation destination. . . .

Start the second paragraph like this:

> Another good destination for your next vacation is _____ . . .

a. Take your ATM card.

b. Enter the amount of cash you want.

c. Take your cash.

d. Put your ATM card in the card slot.

e. Choose your language.

f. Enter your Personal Identification
   Number (PIN).

1 How do you use an ATM machine? Look at the pictures below.
Match each picture with an instruction from the box.

1. ____ 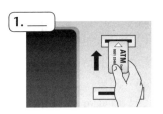   2. ____    3. ____

4. ____    5. ____    6. ____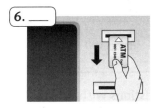

2 Match the financial terms with their definitions. Write the letter on the line.

____ 1. an ATM

____ 2. cash

____ 3. foreign currency

____ 4. a currency exchange

____ 5. an exchange rate

____ 6. a fee

a. money from another country

b. the value of one currency compared to another

c. a machine that you use to get money from your bank account

d. extra charges

e. money in the form of bills or coins (not checks, credit cards, etc.)

f. buying or selling money from another country

3 Answer the questions. Use your own words.

1. "What shop in your city has really nice things?"

   YOU _____

2. "Are things in this shop usually affordable or more than you want to spend?"

   YOU _____

3. "Is it OK to bargain for a lower price in this shop?"

   YOU _____

4. "In your city, where is it OK to bargain?"

   YOU _____

5. "Are you good at bargaining?"

   YOU _____

4 Look at the chart from a digital camera buying guide.

COMPARE DIGITAL CAMERAS				
Brand / Model	**Price**	**Ease of Use**	**Size**	**Weight**
Diego Mini 3000	US$239	●●	c	35 g (1.2 oz)
Honshu B100	US$209	●●●	p	283 g (9.9 oz)
Honshu X24	US$139	●	s	180 g (6.3 oz)
Prego 5	US$299	●●●●	s	135 g (4.7 oz)
Vision 2.0	US$449	●●●	s	224 g (7.9 oz)

KEY

●●●● very easy
●●● pretty easy
●● a little difficult
● difficult

c .... compact (small size, can fit in a shirt pocket)
s .... standard (medium size, similar to a point and shoot camera)
p .... professional (large size, similar to a 35mm camera)

Now write questions with <u>Which</u>. Use the superlative form of the adjectives from the box. For some items, it may be possible to write more than one question.

expensive	light	portable	easy to use	cheap	heavy	difficult to use

1. A: <u>Which camera is the most expensive</u>_____?
   B: The Vision 2.0.

2. A: _____?
   B: The Honshu X24.

3. A: _____?
   B: The Diego Mini 3000.

4. A: _____?
   B: The Prego 5.

5. A: _____?
   B: The Honshu B100.

5 Read each person's statement. For each shopper, recommend a digital camera from the buying guide in Exercise 4. Give a reason for your advice.

"I need a new camera. The one I have now is too heavy. I really want a camera that I can carry in my jacket pocket."

1. (YOU) _____

"I'm looking for a digital camera for my mother. She isn't good with electronics, so it must be very easy to use. What do you recommend?"

2. YOU _____

"I'd like to have a look at your least expensive digital camera. I can't spend more that $150. Do you have anything in my price range?"

3. YOU _____

6 Choose the correct response. Circle the letter.

1. "This camera isn't in my price range."
   a. How much can you spend?
   b. Would you like to take it?
   c. Can I have a look?

2. "Why is this smart phone the best?"
   a. It's the heaviest.
   b. It's the fastest.
   c. It's the most difficult to use.

3. "I can't spend more than $200."
   a. Have a look at our best model.
   b. How would you like to pay for it?
   c. Let me show you something in your price range.

4. "Can I have a look?"
   a. Certainly.
   b. Really?
   c. Excuse me.

7 Complete the conversation. Write the letter on the line.

A: Can I help you?

B: _____
   1.

A: OK. Which one are you interested in?

B: _____
   2.

A: The Muze HD. It's the most popular.

B: _____
   3.

A: What about the XTunes? It's pretty good, and it's more affordable.

B: _____
   4.

A: No. And the sound is great.

B: _____
   5.

A: And how would you like to pay for it?

B: _____
   6.

a. Actually, that's a little out of my price range.

b. Cash, please.

c. Yes, please. I'm looking for an MP3 player for my son.

d. Is it difficult to use?

e. OK. I'll take the XTunes.

f. I don't know. What do you recommend?

8 Complete the sentences. Use _too_ or _enough_ and the adjective.

1. I'm not going to read that book. It's _____ .
   boring
2. Sirena shouldn't travel alone. She isn't _____ .
   old
3. I don't want to buy anything in that shop. The people were _____ .
   unfriendly
4. Talia likes the red rug, but it's _____ for her living room.
   big
5. I love this belt, but it isn't _____ . I need a bigger size.
   long
6. Are your shoes _____ ? We're going to do a lot of walking.
   comfortable
7. We wanted to bargain for a lower price, but it was _____ .
   difficult

9 Complete the conversations. Use words from the box.

too	deal	much	all	low
more	have	bowl	enough	give

A: This _____ is gorgeous. I'd love to get it for my sister.
         1.

B: It's nice. And it's small _____ to take in your suitcase.
                          2.

A: I'm going to ask about the price. I hope it's not _____ expensive.
                                                    3.

• • •

A: I'm interested in this bowl. How _____ do you want for it?
                                    4.

C: This one is $60.

A: That's _____ than I want to spend.
            5.

C: I could go as _____ as $50.
                   6.

A: I can _____ you $30 for it.
          7.

C: You can _____ it for $40. That's a bargain.
             8.

A: _____ I have is $35.
    9.

C: OK. It's a _____ .
                10.

10 Choose the correct response. Write the letter on the line.

_____ 1. "$650! I paid $429 for the same camcorder yesterday!"   a. It can't hurt to ask.

_____ 2. "How much did you pay for that vase?"   b. What a total rip-off!

_____ 3. "Should I try to get a better price?"   c. Thanks. Keep the change.

_____ 4. "I saved a lot of money on this DVD player. It was only $79."   d. What a great deal!

_____ 5. "Here you are, sir. The Atlas Hotel. That's $8.50."   e. Only $20. It was a real
                                                                              bargain.

11 Read the article about bargaining customs around the world.
Then read the statements. Check <u>true</u> or <u>false</u>.

Can you give me a better price?

Bargaining Customs around the World

Bargaining customs are very different around the world. Few would go shopping in another country without knowing the exchange rate. However, many travelers don't learn anything about the local shopping customs of the place they are visiting before spending money. Understanding when it's OK to bargain can save you a lot of money and make your shopping experience much more enjoyable.

In some countries, bargaining is an important part of the shopping culture. In others, bargaining is not done at all. Here's a bargaining guide for some countries around the world:

Morocco: Bargaining is always expected in the shopping markets. Here bargaining is more than just getting the best price. If you go into a shop and agree to the first price a seller offers, the seller may not be happy. For Moroccans, bargaining is a form of entertainment; it's a game of skill, a little bit of acting, and it's a chance to chat about the weather, business, and family. So be sure to have fun and try to get a better price!

New York City: Bargaining is not the custom here. Shop clerks can almost never give you a lower price. However, some hotels may give you a lower rate during the less popular times of year. It can't hurt to ask.

Tahiti: Bargaining is not appropriate in the South Pacific. In fact, it is considered disrespectful to ask for a better price. In the food markets, sellers will even take their fruits and vegetables back home with them, rather than give a discount!

	true	false
1. Bargaining customs are similar around the world.	☐	☐
2. Generally, market sellers in Morocco love to bargain.	☐	☐
3. In New York City, it's OK to bargain for a cheaper hotel room.	☐	☐
4. It can't hurt to ask a fruit seller in Tahiti for a lower price.	☐	☐

12 Read the article on page 116 of the Student's Book again. Then check <u>true</u> or <u>false</u>, according to the article.

EXTRA READING COMPREHENSION

	true	false
1. Tipping is expected in all countries.	☐	☐
2. In U.S. restaurants, a 10% tip is usually enough.	☐	☐
3. In some European countries, you should hand the tip to the waiter.	☐	☐
4. In Germany, you should leave the tip on the table.	☐	☐
5. For a taxi fare of 9.50 pesos in Buenos Aires, give the driver 10 pesos.	☐	☐
6. Australian porters expect a bigger tip than porters in other countries.	☐	☐
7. Tip Japanese porters about US$1 per bag.	☐	☐
8. You should never leave a tip for the housekeeper.	☐	☐

13 Write a short paragraph about bargaining in your own country. What items do people bargain for? What items do people never bargain for?

GRAMMAR BOOSTER

A Complete the chart.

	Adjective	Comparative form	Superlative form
1.	beautiful		
2.			the most intelligent
3.	big		
4.		more convenient	
5.	busy		
6.			the fastest
7.		safer	
8.	noisy		

B Complete the conversations with the comparative or the superlative form of the adjective in parentheses.

1. **A:** Which one of these three sweaters do you think is ___the prettiest___ (pretty)?

   B: The blue one. The other two are not attractive at all.

2. **A:** How do you like the book?

   B: I don't like it. It's _____ (bad) than the one we read last month.

3. **A:** Did you enjoy Australia?

   B: Yes. I think it's one of _____ (interesting) places in the world.

4. **A:** Who is _____ (good) at baseball, you or your brother?

   B: Well, I'm a _____ (fast) base runner, but my brother is a _____ (powerful) hitter. Actually, my dad is _____ (good) player in the family. He was a star player in college.

5. **A:** Which one of the two laptops is _____ (popular)?

   B: Well, the X102 is _____ (cheap) model in the store. But I actually recommend the X200. It's a little _____ (expensive) than the X102, but much _____ (light).

C Answer the questions. Use <u>too</u> or <u>enough</u> and the adjective in parentheses.

1. **A:** Why didn't you buy the tablet?

   B: (expensive) _____ . I need to save money this month.

2. **A:** Is the food too spicy?

   B: (spicy) _____ . I'm going to ask for more hot sauce!

3. **A:** What's wrong with these shoes?

   B: I can't wear them. (uncomfortable) _____ .

4. **A:** Why don't you like the apartment?

   B: (noisy) _____ . I'm looking for a quiet neighborhood.

5. **A:** Why don't you take the train instead of flying?

   B: (fast) _____ . I have to get there as soon as possible.

6. **A:** Do you want to go to a jazz concert?

   B: Thanks for asking, but I'm not a jazz music fan. (boring) _____ .

WRITING BOOSTER

A Rewrite each pair of sentences, using the words in parentheses.

1. This rug is a good deal. It's a bit more than I want to spend. (However)

   This rug is a good deal. However, it's a bit more than I want to spend. _____

2. The Trekker jacket is very warm. It's the lightest one. (even though)

   _____

3. Our new coffee maker is not the most expensive. It makes the best coffee. (However)

   _____

4. Half Moon Café has the best food in town. It's very expensive. (On the other hand)

   _____

5. This is last year's model. The clerk won't give me a lower price. (Even though)

   _____

B Write sentences about the advantages and disadvantages of credit cards and cash. Use the chart on page 111 of the Student's Book. Use <u>Even though</u>, <u>However</u>, and <u>On the other hand</u>.

1. Credit cards: _____

   _____

2. Cash: _____

   _____

C Choose three topics from the list. For each topic, compare their advantages and disadvantages. Use <u>Even though</u>, <u>However</u>, and <u>On the other hand</u>.

> listening to music at home / going to a concert
>
> large family / small family
>
> smart phones / regular cell phones
>
> conservative clothes / wild clothes
>
> air travel / train travel

Listening to music at home is more relaxing. On the other hand, going to a concert is more exciting.

1.

2.

3.

Which continent is home to the world's biggest shopping malls?

It's not North America. Only one of the world's ten largest malls is in the U.S. Built in 1969, the Eastwood Mall Complex in Youngstown, Ohio, is the ninth largest mall. Similarly, one Canadian mall made the top-ten list. The West Edmonton Mall in Alberta, built in 1981, is number six.

Europe's biggest mall—fifth on the list of the world's largest—is newer. It was built in 2005. It's located in Istanbul, Turkey.

The continent with the biggest, newest, and most exciting malls is Asia. Seven of the world's ten largest shopping malls are in Asia. The two largest are in China and opened in 2005 and 2004. The New South China Mall in Dongguan has 1500 stores and 7.1 million square feet of retail space. The Golden Resources Mall in Beijing—also called "The Great Mall of China"—has 50,000 visitors every day. Enormous malls in the Philippines, Dubai, and Malaysia have roller coasters, ice-skating rinks, water parks, aquariums, and bowling alleys.